Born in Adversity

Journeying Victoriously through your Personal Wilderness

BORN IN ADVERSITY

Journeying Victoriously through your Personal Wilderness

E. C. Nakeli

erez
Publishing
Breaking through... Breaking out

Publishing today for tomorrow's generation

© 2012 by E.C. Nakeli

Published by Perez Publishing LLC – *www.perezpublishing.com* –

For your questions and publishing needs write to:
Perez Publishing
548 Congressional Drive
Westminster, MD, 21158
USA
Email: *perezpublishing@gmail.com*

Printed in the United States of America

All rights reserved. No part of this publication may be reproduced, stored in a retrieval system, or transmitted in any form or by any means—for example, electronic, photocopy, recording—without the prior written permission of the publisher. The only exception is brief quotations in printed reviews.

E. C. Nakeli

To contact the author, write to:
E.C. Nakeli
Perez Publishing
548 Congressional Drive
Westminster, MD 21158
USA
Email: *ecnakeli@yahoo.com*

Born in Adversity: Journeying Victoriously Through your Personal Wilderness / E. C. Nakeli

ISBN: 978-0-9850668-4-0

Unless underwise indicated, Scripture references are from
THE HOLY BIBLE, NEW INTERNATIONAL VERSION®, NIV®
Copyright © 1973, 1978, 1984, 2011 by Biblica, Inc.™
Used by permission. All rights reserved worldwide.

Cover Image: © Cardens Design Photography Services, used by permission.

Cover/Interior Design: Zach ESSAMA - *graphicspartner@gmail.com*

Table of Contents

Dedication 7
Acknowledgements 9
Introduction 11

Chapter 1
The Challenge of Growing Up:
A Brief Look at the Life of Isaac 13

Chapter 2
Enduring Unfounded Hatred:
A Brief Look at Joseph 25

Chapter 3
When Life Relegates you into the Desert:
A Brief Look at the Life of Moses 33

Chapter 4
When Life Deprives you of the Basics:
A Look at the Life of Gideon 61

Chapter 5
Thriving in the Midst of Despise and Disdain:
A Brief Look at the Life of David 77

Chapter 6
When you Are Familiar with Sorrow and Suffering:
The Example of Our Lord Jesus 101

Chapter 7
Made by Adversity: A Snapshot at the Life of Paul 119

Chapter 8
You Were Born in Adversity 125

Chapter 9
Some Facts about Adversity 129

Conclusion 137

Dedication

I dedicate this book to my friends and brothers, the Bekondo boys; Plunkert, Kermit, and Enya for braving it through years of adversity. You all braved it through the recent loss of mom and dad, and came out stronger with a greater resolve to face life like the "more than conquerors" you all are. Most especially, I dedicate this book to my very personal friend Kermit. I saw you make it through the long difficult years of your life. Now you seem to be getting a foretaste of your Promised Land. There are many who admire you for who and what you are now without any inkling of how you made it through. I was there when you felt like giving it up in the midst of the ordeals of life, but chose to press on. Your perseverance and dedication to become what God ordained for you, and how you made it through, is a perfect example of those born in adversity.

May the Lord use the words of this book to give hope to those traversing the unavoidable adversities which God uses to make and mold us into the people He wants us to become!

Acknowledgements

I want to acknowledge Epamba Franca for typing the manuscripts, thank you Ayi Mbile for proofreading the work; you are such a great editor. And thank you Zach Essama for your work on the interior design. Many blessings to you all for your tremendous sacrifices! May the voice of your sacrifice speak for you in domains where no other voice is heard, and may you all reap the unique fruit of making a selfless contribution to the success of this project. Thank you to the dedicated staff and members of Perez Publishing for all your efforts to make sound biblical and practical teachings available to this generation. Together we are breaking through and breaking out into new territories, touching lives and fulfilling destinies.

Introduction

Life is a journey that we all undertake. Part of that journey must be done through the wilderness of life. In one way or another, at one moment or another, adversity is bound to come our way. It is our attitude during such moments of adversity that determines the outcome for the rest of our walk. The outcome of what we do during such times of adversity determines the outcome of the rest of our walk. Some have thought it strange that they face adversities in life. It is this strange feeling that has caused many to fail to make it through such times of adversity. My heart goes out to the family of the celebrity sportsman Robert Enke who as a result of depression committed suicide. The story is still making headlines as we are writing this introduction.

Like him, many have forfeited their destiny through suicide or by far reaching compromises as a means of escape from the pain of going through the indispensable desert years. In this little book, we want to, by the power of the Holy Spirit offer hope to those who may be going through their own personal wilderness. The questions we seek to ask ourselves are: what are the causes of adversity? Do adversities have a purpose? How can I survive my time of adversity?

Are there some nuggets to help me navigate my wilderness? The best place to draw inspiration is from the lives of those who've been through adversities and came out victoriously. For that reason we will turn to God's handbook of life and draw inspiration from the timeless stories embedded throughout its pages.

We will examine the lives of some Bible characters who made it through their seasons of adversity and not only came out whole or unscathed but more importantly better off than they were before they traversed their individual deserts. It doesn't matter what the wilderness is that you are going through at this time. One thing I do know is that after every wilderness comes the Promised Land. It is our attitude in seasons of adversity which determines how soon we step into the Promised Land that lies just ahead. The way you handle your wilderness days will determine the course of your life thereafter.

My prayer is that God will use the words and stories in this book to bring renewed hope to the despairing and disillusioned. May He use these words to transform battered, shattered and haggard lives, and give rest in the midst of turmoil! May He cause His glory to shine forth in healing and restoration of shattered hopes and broken dreams!

Finally, know that you were born in adversity. This will put you in a position of victory and triumph. May you learn to use your adversities as stepping stones rather than stumbling blocks!

Chapter 1

The Challenge of Growing Up: A Brief Look at the Life of Isaac

Isaac was a child of promise born in adversity. The womb that carried him was a womb that knew adversity until God's intervention. Sarah had given up all hope of ever nursing a child. She endured the mockery of her relatives, neighbors, and servants. In a desperate attempt to do herself justice she gave her slave girl to her husband to make a family for herself. Finally at God's own time she brought forth a son and said, *"God has brought me laughter, and everyone who hears about this will laugh with me"* (Genesis 21:6). This means Sarah had lived her life all these years without any joy. Laughter eluded her; shame and mockery were like her necklace. No doubt she brought forth an Ishmael through Hagar.

Sometimes we are pushed to look for human solutions in the face of adversity. And such solutions end up aggravating the situation at hand like it did for Sarah.

HOSTILITY IN HIS CHILDHOOD

9 But Sarah saw that the son whom Hagar the Egyptian had borne to Abraham was mocking, 10 and she said to Abraham, "Get rid of that slave woman and her son, for that slave woman's son will never share in the inheritance with my son Isaac."
(Genesis 21:9-10)

Even in his childhood, Isaac started experiencing the hostility of his environment. The kind of hostility the mother experienced before he was born. Ishmael took upon himself to mock, ridicule, and torment the tender soul of the young lad Isaac. I am very convinced it is something that went on for long without Sarah ever noticing. Maybe Ishmael gathered the children of the servants to mock and ridicule little Isaac each time Sarah wasn't on guard.

There are children born like this into very hostile environments. Maybe it is a condition of quarrelling and fighting between the parents. The tender soul of many a child faces untold torment in the hostility of the home instead of the love it needs to experience. To an extent this may go a long way to affect the child at a later stage in life if not properly handled. Things babies and little children hear get encoded in their spiritual genetics and influence them in one way or the other. I do know what Ishmael said and what he did to mock at Isaac, but this time around Sarah took note. And I want to believe it was not

The Challenge of Growing Up: A Brief Look at the Life of Isaac

the first time. If it were she couldn't have insisted that both Hagar and Ishmael be sent away. Whatever the case the bottom line is Isaac faced adversity even at a very tender age.

You may be in a family, a neighbourhood or an office where you are subject to mockery, ridicule and shame, for one reason or another. You may have grown up in a hostile environment where for the greater part the people around you were actively or passively hostile to you. Do not be dismayed, you are just one among many born in adversity. Your own adversity should not be viewed as a predicament. If you view it as a predicament you may develop hatred for those who were used to bring about the adverse circumstances that surround you. Rather view it as a means used by your creator to bring out the champion in you.

THE SACRIFICIAL LAMB

*9*When they reached the place God had told him about, Abraham built an altar there and arranged the wood on it. He bound his son Isaac and laid him on the altar, on top of the wood. *10* Then he reached out his hand and took the knife to slay his son. *11* But the angel of the LORD called out to him from heaven, "Abraham! Abraham!" "Here I am," he replied.

(Genesis 22:9-11)

Isaac's adverse circumstances did not end when he was just a little child. As a teenager, even his own father "turned" against him at the command of God. Isaac was to be sacrificed. In hostility he was bound, hands, feet and all. In hostility he was put on the wooden altar. I can imagine the thorny portion of the wood piercing and pricking him as he lay there helpless.

The father was not acting. He was ready to slay him and set the fire underneath. But for the intervention of the Lord, Isaac's life would have ended in the hands of his own father.

There are some of you out there who have at one time or another, or are in the process of experiencing hostility from your own parents. You have been born in adversity. I want to counsel you not to become hostile towards your father or mother. After this hostile episode with his father, Isaac remained obedient to Abraham. Isaac did not go to the servants to expose what Abraham had done and attempted on him. The reason, I believe, why many people do not receive the blessing and promotion that usually comes after adverse circumstances is because they react negatively when faced with adversity. May be for you it's not a father's hostility, or a mother's hostility, but that of a sweetheart.

It is sad to see that lovers can become so hostile one to another. Sometimes it is one party that suffers the hostility. If you are the one experiencing such hostility, I want to counsel you to not react with hostility. Isaac did not retaliate. He did not plan to revenge on his father when he was old. Oh! How my heart goes out to some elderly men and women who are experiencing real hostility at the hands of their own offspring who think the parent(s) had maltreated them when they were young.

> *Is your heart right towards your father and mother? Are you maintaining a right attitude towards that relative in whose hands you grew up?*

What about that teacher or senior student who may have treated you unpleasantly, have you corrected your heart towards that one?

ABIMELECH'S HOSTILITY

Isaac by now was a grown man, with a wife of his own and two children. The father and mother were now of blessed memory. Famine broke in the land and Isaac experienced the pinch of the famine. He left and went down to Gerah among the philistines. Even there the famine was greatly felt and he attempted to go down to Egypt. It is at this point the Lord appeared to him and asked him to not go down to Egypt but to stay in Gerah.

Isaac had a choice, to look at the famine and its effect on him and his family and to go to Egypt or to obey the voice of God and stay in the midst of the famine. Listen; sometimes in adverse situations you will always have the option to react in the natural that is, according to your instincts or to obey God's voice. I do not know what kind of famine you are in, but even in that adverse condition, God is saying something to you. When you are born in adversity, do not seek a solution from the world. For every adverse condition that surrounds you, God's voice has the answer. Isaac, however, chose to obey God. This meant he had to continue to feel the pinch of the famine, together with his family. It was a tough time for Isaac. I want to believe Rebecca could not understand, the boys could not understand him, but he chose to obey the voice of God. And of course God rewarded his obedience by blessing what he sowed so that his harvest was a hundredfold. It is this hundredfold blessing that provoked the jealousy and eventual hostility of Abimelech. The Philistines sought to destroy his flocks and the easiest way was for them to deprive them of water. They proceeded to stop all the wells he had uncovered. This was a clear sign to Isaac that he was no longer welcomed in that place. Sometimes, those hostile to you will send their message across in different ways. Sometimes it is just in their attitude, and you need discernment to know. About Jacob when he was in the home of his uncle-turned father-in-law, the Bible says, *"And Jacob noticed that Laban's attitude towards him was not what it had been"* (Genesis 31:2). Jacob was not told, he only was observant enough to notice. Those who must survive the hostility of their environment would be those who are observant. It will be those who possess the spirit of discernment. Those who are able to see and read beyond surface actions.

After active, non-verbal hostility of stopping every well Isaac dug, Abimelech proceeded to make his feelings known to Isaac.

When Men Send you away

12 Isaac planted crops in that land and the same year reaped a hundredfold, because the LORD blessed him. *13* The man became rich, and his wealth continued to grow until he became very wealthy. *14* He had so many flocks and herds and servants that the Philistines envied him. *15* So all the wells that his father's servants had dug in the time of his father Abraham, the Philistines stopped up, filling them with earth.

16 Then Abimelech said to Isaac, "Move away from us; you have become too powerful for us."

(Genesis 26:12-16)

The Challenge of Growing Up: A Brief Look at the Life of Isaac

Isaac did nothing wrong to deserve such a treatment. The only cause of this hostility was the blessing God had poured into his lap. Listen, I have often said those who expect to be at peace with everybody are not ready for God's blessings. When God blesses you, the hostile thoughts of your foes in the cloak of friends will be manifested in words and eventual actions. You do not have to do anything wrong for people to become hostile towards you. Sometimes your only crime is that you are standing out. You may be standing out and standing tall. You may be standing out in blessing. You may be standing out in zeal. You may be standing out in love. You may be standing out in generosity. You may be standing out in holiness. The truth is that we are in a world which encourages unwholesome squeezing into the mold of mediocrity. Hence anyone who dares to stand out becomes a target of gossip, slander, calumny, hatred, and animosity. It is at such a time when many give up their pursuits and exploits which made them stand out from the crowd as a means to escape hostility. Isaac understood he was destined to stand out in blessing and thus was willing to bear the anger of jealous men and women.

Relentless Adversity

Abimelech asked Isaac to move away, and Isaac obeyed and moved away into the valley. I don't know where or what you have been driven from, and by whom, may be from your home, job, business, or ministry. The intention of those who drove you out was to deprive you of the joy, blessing, success, or happiness you may be enjoying. They think it's because of them you are what you are. The truth is, God will use their hostility for your promotion. God will use this to show them that He El-Shaddai, and not them, is the source of your blessing, joy, happiness, and success. It is an opportunity for Him to show Himself mighty on your behalf and demonstrate the fact that He can make you become whatever He has ordained for you to become irrespective of the actions of your haters.

To show that Isaac was born in adversity and for adversity, the hostility followed him into the valley he moved into. The Bible says, *"19 Isaac's servants dug in the valley and discovered a well of fresh water there. 20 But the herdsmen of Gerar quarreled with Isaac's herdsmen and said, «The water is ours!» So he named the well Esek, because they disputed with him. 21 Then they dug another well, but they quarreled over that one also; so he named it Sitnah."* (Genesis 26:19-21)

May be your live is filled and surrounded with internal disputes and external hostilities and oppositions. Everywhere Isaac turned at this point in time, he faced hostility. To the left he met with disputes of various kinds. To the right he met with varied forms of opposition from his environment. Isn't it funny that hostilities just seem to come relentlessly? You turn to your right and there is this problem. You turn to your left and there is this other issue. Before you trouble is approaching on the horizon, behind you it is brewing like a hot beverage and you are caught between a rock and a hard place. It is at such a time when your dawn is closest. So just keep hanging in there and do not give up.

However, there came a time when, *"He moved on from there and dug another well, and no one quarreled over it. He named it Rehoboth, saying, «Now the LORD has given us room and we will flourish in the land»"* (Genesis 26:22). Each time, the hostility of his environment was pushing him to a more spacious place. Unknowingly, they were driving him to the place where he would flourish. Listen to me, most often before you ever reach your Rehoboth (room) you must have passed through Esek (dispute) and Sitnar (opposition). And often, Rehoboth (room) is just for you to reach your Beersheba – the place of your God encounter.

> *23* From there he went up to Beersheba. *24* That night the LORD appeared to him and said, "I am the God of your father Abraham. Do not be afraid, for I am with you; I will bless you and will increase the number of your descendants for the sake of my servant Abraham."
> *25* Isaac built an altar there and called on the name of the LORD. There he pitched his tent, and there his servants dug a well.
> (Genesis 26:23-25)

For the first time in Isaac's life we are told he built an altar to God. Before now, he had depended on his father's relationship with God and all that he accomplished as a result of God's blessing on him. Adversity is meant to take you deeper in your relationship with God. It comes to drive and push you forward. It is meant to increase your resolve to pursue excellence. There comes a time when hostility gives up on the one who has refused to give up. The rest of the story tells us that everything worked in the favour of Isaac. His enemies who had been hostile came and sought peace with Isaac. If you remain faithful to Bible principles in the face of adversity, God will surely show up in your favor. And things will turn for your favor. You may be asking for how long it has to be this way. I tell you as long as the hostility lasts, maintain the right attitude. Those who drove you away will come looking for you. Those who hated you will seek your favor. Your being born in adversity is not a predicament but a school to prepare you for God's abundance. Just as hostility was part of Isaac's life, abundance was also part of his life. The thing is many people in studying Isaac, concentrated on the abundance of his life while ignoring the hostility he was subject to.

Adversity produced in him the capacity to endure, elevation amongst his peers, and a deeper relationship with God.

Summary

✤ Sometimes we are pushed to look for human solutions in the face of adversity. And such solutions end up aggravating the situation at hand like it did for Sarah.

✤ The reason, I believe, why many people do not receive the blessing and promotion that usually comes after adverse circumstances is because they react negatively when faced with adversity.

✤ Sometimes in adverse situations you will always have the option to react in the natural that is, according to your instincts or to obey God's voice.

✤ For every adverse condition that surrounds you, God's voice has the answer.

✤ Those hostile to you will send their message across in different ways. Sometimes it is just in their attitude, and you need discernment to know.

✤ You do not have to do anything wrong for people to become hostile towards you. Sometimes your only crime is that you are standing out.

✤ Isaac understood he was destined to stand out in blessing and thus was willing to bear the anger of jealous men and women for Him to show Himself.

- He can make you become whatever He has ordained for you to become irrespective of the actions of your haters.

- Most often before you ever reach your Rehoboth (room) you must have passed through Esek (dispute) and Sitnar (opposition).

- Adversity is meant to take you deeper in your relationship with God. It comes to drive and push you forward.

- There comes a time when hostility gives up on the one who has refused to give up.

- If you remain faithful to Bible principles in the face of adversity, God will surely show up in your favor. And things will turn for your favor.

- Your being born in adversity is not a predicament but a school to prepare you for God's abundance.

- Adversity produced in him the capacity to endure, elevation amongst his peers, and a deeper relationship with God.

Chapter 2

Enduring Unfounded Hatred: A Brief Look at Joseph

Joseph was born into a polygamous home of intense rivalry between his mother and her sister who had become the wives of Jacob. Not only was there rivalry between the women but also between Rachael (Joseph's mother) and her husband whom she blamed for her childlessness. His mother had lived with the *"disgrace"* of barrenness for such a long time that when Joseph was conceived and eventually born, she said, *"God has taken away my disgrace"*. She therefore treasured Joseph and poured all of her love into him. It is this deep love of the parents for Joseph and the consequent favors that caused his brothers to hate him with such intense hatred.

In the Midst of Verbal Adversity

The Bible says,

> *3* Now Israel loved Joseph more than any of his other sons, because he had been born to him in his old age; and he made a richly ornamented robe for him. *4* When his brothers saw that their father loved him more than any of them, they hated him and could not speak a kind word to him.
>
> (Genesis 37:3-4)

I do not know the way the people around you are treating you. May be you are hated not because of what you have done but because of God's special favor on you. May be you are going through some form of disdain and despise from a group of people not because you have hurt them in any way but because of the love others are showering on you. You may have been endowed with special abilities and there are some who hate you for that. You may be the object of someone's special love and favor and some have hated you for that. I want you to see that in the case of Joseph, his brothers' hatred was not passive but it was an active hatred. *"They hated him and could not speak a kind word to him"*. This means every word that came from their mouth addressed to Joseph was unkind.

They cussed, fused, raved, raged and ranted at him all the time. They cursed, ridiculed and insulted Joseph all the time. It is in such a hostile environment that Joseph grew up. May be you have been the subject of verbal hostility. May be because of your Christian stance your boss or relatives have never spoken a kind word to you or about you. May be you have found special God-given favor before those who matter and those who do not matter have raised a verbal assault on you. Do not fret; their words cannot change anything about you if you refuse to take offence. It is when you take offence that you are affected negatively. Some times to survive in such a hostile environment of verbal assault you will have to give a deaf ear to the negative things said about you. The fact that you were born in adversity cannot be changed. But the effects of the adverse circumstances on your destiny are determined by you. You can view them as a pointer to God's special plan for your life or you can allow them break you down. It is very easy for verbal assaults, especially when persistently from those in your immediate surroundings, to have a negative toll on one. That is why you must refuse to drink them it. And you do so by refusing to allow your mind to dwell on such. There is no way Joseph could have fared well if he had reacted negatively to the hostility and hatred of his brothers.

As if the hatred, because he was loved, was not enough, when he had his dream and shared it with his brothers, they hated him all the more for it. *"His brothers said to him, «Do you intend to reign over us? Will you actually rule us?» And they hated him all the more because of his dream and what he had said."* (Genesis 37:8)

I do not know what your dreams are, but understand that as you work to accomplish your dreams, it will separate the ranks between your friends and fiends. When Joseph shared his second dream, *"His brothers were jealous of him, but his father kept the matter in mind."*

In the same way expect the ranks to be separated between those who will cherish and support you and those who will be jealous and hate you, those who will pray for you and those who will pray against you.

SEEN IN A DISTANCE

18 But they saw him in the distance, and before he reached them, they plotted to kill him.

19 "Here comes that dreamer!" they said to each other. *20* "Come now, let's kill him and throw him into one of these cisterns and say that a ferocious animal devoured him. Then we'll see what comes of his dreams."

(Genesis 37:18-20)

I want to believe Joseph was already deeply aware of the animosity of his brothers toward him. However, his loyalty to his father and love for his brothers made him vulnerable to their plot. In the same light many people suffer hostility because of the Christian love they are called to show. Because of their loyalty to their heavenly Father's cause some are enduring the most hostile environments. You are born in adversity. Every believer in Christ is. I will dwell more on this in a later chapter.

I want you to take special note of verse 18, it says, *"But they saw him in a distance, and before he reached them, the plotted to kill him."*

Every child of destiny has been seen in a distance by the forces of evil. These forces have plotted your ruin before you reach your goal. They have seen God's deposit in your life and have vowed that you will not accomplish God's purpose for your life. I want you to understand that the fact that you are born in adversity means that your pathway is concealed with traps, pits, snares and nets from the enemy. All these are to see what becomes of God's purpose for your life. The world you live in is a hostile world; hostile towards God, towards His people, and towards His purpose for your life. You must live conscious of the fact that you are born in adversity so that you can avoid the unnecessary snares the evil one has concealed on the pathway to your destiny. Joseph's enemies said, *"Come now, let's kill him and throw him into one of these cisterns and say that a ferocious animal devoured him. Then we'll see what comes of his dreams."* The goal of their hostility was to see what became of Joseph's dreams. And that is what the enemy is out for, to see what becomes of the dreams you have. Everything he sends your way is with the goal to bring about a miscarriage to your dreams and purpose in life. But the good news is that the Almighty, omniscient, omnipotent God uses the adversities of life and the ill intentions of the devil to bring into fulfilment the dreams He placed in the inside of you. May the Lord open your eyes to, and grant you divine wisdom to deal with, the traps and snares of the enemy on the pathway to your destiny.

Even for Joseph, his brothers' hatred and betrayal pushed him into experiencing God's presence and preservation. In every situation of betrayal, the Bible lets us know that *"God was with Joseph and he prospered."*

His ultimate betrayal that paved the way for his ascent into glory was that of his master's wife. And that because of Joseph's integrity! I wrote very comprehensively on Joseph in my book *"Storms and Flames of Glory"* and I will not like to repeat myself here. It suffices to say that Joseph's life was down and down until God's time came. He went down to the pit, down to Egypt and down to prison.

May be your life has been going down and down. You wonder when things will ever start going up. Listen to me, you can work to change things you can change. But there are things in life which you cannot change. In such a case being anxious and worrying about them will only give you heartache and more headaches thereby reducing your capacity to concentrate.

Do you find yourself in a pit? Have you been sold out by those you have trusted for years? Do you find yourself unjustly thrown into a prison? Whatever the situation, God is with you and will cause you to prosper if you will trust Him and give Him charge of your affairs. You can prosper even in the heat of adversity. Adversity comes to provoke the hidden virtues in you to be made manifest. Adversity comes to raise you to your best.

Summary

* The fact that you were born in adversity cannot be changed. But the effects of the adverse circumstances on your destiny are determined by you.

* As you work to accomplish your dreams, it will separate the ranks between your friends and fiends.

* Expect the ranks to be separate between those who will cherish and support you and those who will be jealous and hate you, those who will pray for you and those who will pray against you.

* Many people suffer hostility because of the Christian love they are called to show. Because of their loyalty to their heavenly Father's cause some are enduring the most hostile environment.

* Every child of destiny has been seen in a distance by the forces of evil.

* The fact that you are born in adversity means that your pathway is concealed with traps, pits, snares and nets from the enemy. All these are to see what becomes of God's purpose for your life.

* You must live conscious of the fact that you are born in adversity so that you can avoid the unnecessary

snares the evil one has concealed on the pathway to your destiny.

* And that is what the enemy is out for, to see what becomes of the dreams you have. Everything he sends your way is with the goal to bring about a miscarriage to your dreams and purpose in life.

* The Almighty, omniscient, omnipotent God uses the adversities of life and the ill intentions of the devil to bring into fulfilment the dreams He placed in the inside of you.

* For Joseph, his brothers' hatred and betrayal pushed him into experiencing God's presence and preservation.

* Joseph's life was down and down until God's time came. He went down to the pit, down to Egypt and down to prison.

* Adversity comes to provoke the hidden virtues in you to be made manifest. Adversity comes to raise you to your best.

Chapter 3

When Life Relegates you into the Desert: A Brief Look at the Life of Moses

It is the story of Moses that gave me the idea of this book. It is indeed the story of a man born not only in adversity, it seems, but born for adversity. His was a life surrounded by, and greatly influenced by adversity.

BORN INTO OPPRESSION

Like I mentioned a few lines ago, the story of Moses is one littered with adversity. By the time he was born, the thriving Israelites in Egypt had been converted to slaves. The Egyptian oppression of the people of God was very cruel. In spite of such cruelty the Israelites multiplied and spread in all directions in the land. It is written that, *"But the more they were oppressed, the more they multiplied and spread; so the Egyptians came to dread the Israelites."* (Exodus 1:12) It seems to me these guys were designed to thrive in adversity. You see, there are many people who can only excel under adverse circumstances. You take away the adversity and they are reduced to nothing. I call such people those designed for adversity. There are others who will thrive in any condition, adversity or no adversity and their whole physical, psychological and emotional build-up is designed to adapt to different circumstances. There are others who crumble and are crumpled under the least pressure. Such cannot and will never grow deeper in life because pressure increases with depth. The greater the responsibility you are called to carry in life the greater the pressure you will encounter in life. The Israelites were God's chosen people, through whom the whole world had to be blessed. And the enemies to God's purpose put them under the heat of oppression so as to frustrate God's purpose. But in doing so they were actually paving the way for their exodus and eventual inheritance of the Promise Land.

It is at that height of the Egyptian oppression of the Israelites that Moses was born. He was born at a time when all male children of the Israelites had to be thrown to die. The King's edict said, *"Every boy that is born you must throw into the Nile…"* (Exodus 1:22)

BORN IN ADVERSITY

1 Now a man of the house of Levi married a Levite woman, *2* and she became pregnant and gave birth to a son. When she saw that he was a fine child, she hid him for three months. *3* But when she could hide him no longer, she got a papyrus basket for him and coated it with tar and pitch. Then she placed the child in it and put it among the reeds along the bank of the Nile. *4* His sister stood at a distance to see what would happen to him.

5 Then Pharaoh's daughter went down to the Nile to bathe, and her attendants were walking along the river bank. She saw the basket among the reeds and sent her slave girl to get it. *6* She opened it and saw the baby. He was crying, and she felt sorry for him. "This is one of the Hebrew babies," she said.

(Exodus 2:1-6)

Moses was indeed born in adversity. At birth there was already a death sentence on his life, simply because he was an Israelite male child. It was nothing of his making.

There are people born into adversity because of their race. Some, because of their ethnicity, others because of their tribe, and still others because of their family background. Adversity is hardly the making of the one facing it. I do not know the cause of the adversity you were born in. Whatever the reason you can use the adversity to become what God ordained for you from before the foundations of the world. Adversity is like chisel in the hand of a craftsman to cut away the unwanted portions and trim the rough edges, thereby bringing out the artwork.

Moses never knew the joy babies feel when they are celebrated into a family because he had to be hidden. There was no cause of celebration by the parents because that would have meant losing their boy. *"When she saw that he was a fine child, she hid him for three months"*.

Sometimes very ugly things happen to beautiful people. Bad things happen to good people. Hate comes to loving people. Adversity does not look at your face or form sometimes.

It comes knocking at any door any time. Have you ever ask yourself sometimes why bad things happen to good people? I have asked that question myself but haven't found the perfect answer yet. The best way to handle adversity is to prepare for it by making up your mind in advance that nothing will ever knock you out. You may be knocked down once in a while but never be knocked out by adversity. Making up your mind gives you staying power in the midst of storms.

You Can't Help God

Moses' mother did her best to preserve the life of her fine child but she could only go as far as three months.

Can I be honest with you? Human efforts to avoid adversity can only be short lived. There comes situations when human help and ideas become utterly useless. There came a time when Moses' mother could hide him no longer. She came to the end of her road! Have you reached a dead end in life? Have you gotten to a place where human wisdom has nothing to contribute? Have you reached a place where your best efforts amount to nothing? It happened to Jochebed, and all she could do was design a basket into which to put her son.

While other male children were being thrown into the Nile, Moses was placed in a basket well coated and put in the Nile. The basket was kept afloat around the same place along the bank where it was placed thanks to the reeds. Listen; when God's hand is on your life, that place where people are drowning will be the same place where you will be preserved. The place which is the grave yard to many a vision will be the gateway to your rising to the palace. While others perished in the water Moses was drawn out of it into the palace.

Don't you see that it's a miracle you are still sound and standing up? There are many whose lives have become dysfunctional just by going through a fraction of what you have been through this far. This is a sign to you that God's hand is upon your life. You can still lift your hands and bless His name. You can still confess the fact that He is Lord and sovereign. All these are signs that God's hand is still holding you. Why don't you lift up your hands now and give Him praise because adversity has not, and will not consume you?

The Secret to Living Victoriously

As a child of God you must understand that God has arranged your steps and stops. If you live a consecrated and surrendered life, what ultimately happens to your life is determined by God Himself. When God's hand is on you dead ends become bridges to the next stage of your life. Stumbling blocks become stepping stones to your destiny. Adversities become springboards to your God-ordained heights.

There came a time when Moses' Mother could no longer shield him from the adverse circumstances that awaited him. There is a time when you have to rise up to life's challenges or go down permanently. If you must survive adversity you must learn to take the bull by the horn.

I do not know for how long baby Moses suffered from the up and down movements of his basket caused by the ripples from the river motion. I don't know the damage the river current was already causing to the basket. One thing is certain; God knows when to close the curtains on each episode of trials. He arranged for Pharaoh's daughter to pull Moses out of water so he could be taken care of, not in hiding this time but in the open, provided for by the palace, yes at the expense of the very one who passed an edict against his life. God in deed prepares a table before His own in the presence of their enemies.

REJECTED BY HIS OWN PEOPLE

*11*One day, after Moses had grown up, he went out to where his own people were and watched them at their hard labor. He saw an Egyptian beating a Hebrew, one of his own people. *12* Glancing this way and that and seeing no one, he killed the Egyptian and hid him in the sand. *13* The next day he went out and saw two Hebrews fighting. He asked the one in the wrong, "Why are you hitting your fellow Hebrew?"

14 The man said, "Who made you ruler and judge over us? Are you thinking of killing me as you killed the Egyptian?" Then Moses was afraid and thought, "What I did must have become known."*15* When Pharaoh heard of this, he tried to kill Moses, but Moses fled from Pharaoh and went to live in Midian, where he sat down by a well.

(Exodus 2:11-15)

Though Moses was in the palace, in the midst of all the luxury and comfort, psychologically he was in torment as he saw his own people oppressed. This led to a build-up of anger and resentment towards the Egyptians. The pressure on him was so great that he decided to provide a human solution to a divinely permitted, (and would I say orchestrated?) problem. And this is where many people blow it. They seek a natural solution to a problem which is supernatural in origin. In doing so, they get themselves deeper into the mire. Moses was passionate about setting his people free. His passion for freedom was right but his method was wrong as the Israelites could be of no match to their Egyptian slave owners. When Moses intervened in love and concern to rescue his people, he thought he was going to be celebrated. What he met with was rejection, anger, and betrayal.

"Who Made you Ruler and Judge over us?"

I know somebody reading this has faced one form of this question or another. You have sought the wellbeing of some people who have accused you of trying to rule over them. Rejection is a problem to many people. Some have developed mental illnesses because of the impact of rejection. Rejection has pushed many to the brink of suicide. Others could not handle it and have fallen over the edge of the cliff. Some children have turned into monsters because of the pain of rejection. You may be passing through one form of rejection or another. May be your spouse has rejected you. May be you are facing the rejection of your parents, extended relatives or even your own children. Whatever the form rejection takes, its effects can be damaging. I don't know for how long you have bled through the wound of rejection. But I want you to know that God cares and His loving arms are wide open to embrace you. It seems to me that until a man or woman, boy or girl has been rejected by men; such a one does not fully feel accepted by God. Human rejection usually paves the way to discovering the privilege to be accepted in the beloved.

Are you earmarked for greatness? Rejection is the pathway. Before you are celebrated you will first be rejected. As I have studied the lives of God's great leaders in the Bible, and even contemporaries, I have seen that Rejection Land has been an obligatory stop for most if not all of them. If you find yourself going through Rejection Land at this time in your life I want you to put on the coat of trust. Let your eyes be lifted up to God's holy hill. Focus on the Lord and let Him be your shield. Knowing that God is your companion and building that relationship is the only guarantee of making it sanely through Rejection Land. If not you will slip into the pit of anger, resentment and ultimately fall into the ravine of depression.

There are some who have reacted to rejection by building around them a tight cocoon that keeps others at arm's length. The fear of further rejection has caused them to shun the company, let alone companionship of others.

Do you find yourself wrapped up in such a cocoon?

Do you find yourself having slipped into the ravine of depression because you were going through rejection? I challenge you this day by the Word of God to break open that cocoon. I challenge you to climb your way out of the ravine by seeking inner healing. That cocoon is the reason you cannot enjoy life. Once it gets broken, life will be full of meaning once again. Breaking it demands courage and God is willing to impart to you the courage you need if you ask Him in all sincerity. Such cocoons of self-defence limit what you can benefit from others and how far you can see or grow. Break it by all means and expand your horizon in life. I challenge you to enter your freedom this day; freedom from the effects of rejection. Freedom from the fear of rejection. O! That the arm of the Lord God of hosts will reach out and pull you out of the ravine to the surface of the radiance of God's companionship.

HAVE YOU BEEN BETRAYED?

"Are you thinking of killing me as you killed the Egyptian?"

Sometimes, there are things we do, known only to those we consider dear to us. They are people of our own inner circle of relationships and so we hope the secret remains a secret. Sometimes we have had to confide in someone we trust and hope our confidence is upheld whatever the situation. I need not say life does not always offer what we think or desire. We are often presented on silver platters with that which we never would for a second have desired.

Moses left the comfort of the palace he was in to be around those who were dear to his heart. He saw an Egyptian mistreating his own countryman and decided to risk it all to protect his people. In his passion to see freedom for his people, Moses actually committed murder and hid his victim in the sand. He was convinced that no one had witnessed what he had done. Even if anyone did it was of the people whose interest he sought with all his heart.

Are there some skeletons in your wardrobe?

Is there a corpse you have hidden in the sand of your heart? Is someone a murder victim of your intense hatred and resentment?

You may not have committed outright murder but did the Lord Jesus not say hatred in the heart is tantamount to murder?

Clean up your Life

Are there some things about you which you wish no one knows about? Are there some reptiles in the swamp of your unconfessed and unexposed past? It is these monsters we rare in the swamp of our un-confessed and unexposed pasts that hunt us and sting us when we least expect. Sometimes confession is incomplete until exposure to a necessary authority is carried out. When this is done, the enemy's ground for accusation is cut out from beneath him. There is one thing which is sure. If you cover your sin, no matter how deep in the sand of life, one day, that sin will find you out. The sin which has not been exposed will find you out. Secrecy preserves sins instead of destroying them. No matter how long it takes, until the necessary restitution is carried out the sin will continue to exist and at the opportune time will raise its ugly head to hunt its victim.

Let's get back to Moses. He was dead earnest in what he did. He was consumed by the passion of liberation of his own people. When he did what he did, he was making a choice *"to be ill-treated along with the people of God rather than to enjoy the pleasures of sin for a short time"*. (Hebrews 11:25)

NOT LIKE HE THOUGHT

23 When Moses was forty years old, he decided to visit his fellow Israelites. *24* He saw one of them being mistreated by an Egyptian, so he went to his defense and avenged

> him by killing the Egyptian. **25** Moses thought that his own people would realize that God was using him to rescue them, but they did not. **26** The next day Moses came upon two Israelites who were fighting. He tried to reconcile them by saying, "Men, you are brothers; why do you want to hurt each other?"
>
> **27** But the man who was mistreating the other pushed Moses aside and said, "Who made you ruler and judge over us? **28** Do you want to kill me as you killed the Egyptian yesterday?" **29** When Moses heard this, he fled to Midian, where he settled as a foreigner and had two sons.
>
> (Acts 7:23-29)

Moses actually least expected to be rejected and betrayed by his own people. When he took matters in his hands, he actually expected to be accepted and celebrated by the people to whose rescue he had come. After all he was known as the powerful prince in Egypt. He was known to have left the comfort of Pharaoh's palace for the discomfort of the field of slavery.

I am quite sure Moses story was known amongst the Hebrews. His stay in the palace for that long had actually built up resentment in the hearts of some. He was thought to be indifferent to their suffering. There are people who think God has planned for us to take the same path in life. Sometimes you are rejected and betrayed not because of anything you have done but because God has arranged a different path for you from that of the majority. People may reject and betray you because they think you do not feel the hurt they feel. They may treat you shamefully because you enjoy certain privileges they do not.

Many times people will not always treat you or react to your help the way you think. Some will be grateful. Others will react negatively. Others will accuse you of one thing or another.

Moses, instead of being celebrated and acclaimed was rejected and betrayed. His enemies were the members of his household – his own countryman. May be you have been betrayed by someone dear to your heart. It may be a spouse. It may be a child. It may be a trusted friend. Whatever the case you feel deeply hurt and heartbroken.

You have been sold out and you do not know where to turn to. May be you are saying, at least Moses had a Midian to run to but there is nowhere for you to run. What you whispered in secret is now being proclaimed from the roof tops. I want to let you know even your betrayals are an enrolment in God's school of training. Sometimes until you are betrayed you cannot be fully and truly celebrated. Your betrayals are setting you up for a God-encounter. Every betrayal takes you closer your mount Horeb if you will refuse to harbour anger and resentment against those who betray you.

A PATHWAY TO BROKENNESS

The rejections and betrayals you experience in life are working in you the much needed brokenness if ever you are to be used by God. It is written that, *"Moses was educated in all the wisdom of the Egyptians and was powerful in speech and action."* (Acts 7:22)

Take a look at the worldly qualifications of Moses:

i. Educated in all the wisdom of the Egyptians;
ii. Powerful in speech;
iii. Powerful in action;

By inference:

iv. Lived in the luxury of the Egyptian Palace, and according to history;
v. Was a captain in the Egyptian army.

With all these credentials, there was every reason for Moses to have thought that he was God's man for the liberation of God's people. Surely he was, but not for any of the above reasons. For we read that,

> **26** Brothers and sisters, think of what you were when you were called. Not many of you were wise by human standards; not many were influential; not many were of noble birth. **27** But God chose the foolish things of the world to shame the wise; God chose the weak things of the world to shame the strong. **28** God chose the lowly things of this world and the despised things—and the things that are not—to nullify the things that are, **29** so that no one may boast before him.
>
> (1Corinthians 1:26-29)

As a result of the betrayal Moses got enrolled in God's school of humiliation, in order to workout humility in him. The pride of the Egyptian palace, education, military training and all what not had to be knocked out of Him. And it took God forty long years to accomplish that in him.

Two Worlds Apart

Do you know what it means to be driven from the comfort of a king's Palace into the discomfort of the heat of the desert? Do you know what it means to have the dead sentence over your head for forty years? Do you know what it means to live as a fugitive for half of your life?

From the palace to the desert!
From a revered prince to a shepherd!
From a self-proclaimed liberator to a fugitive!
Can you see God's strong hand upon His man?

Just like Moses was a fugitive from pharaoh, there are many people hiding in plain sight. Some are hiding from the realities of life, others are hiding from their past mistakes they've failed to deal with, still others are hiding from themselves and the challenges life offers. Yet there are some who are hiding from God. Are you a fugitive in any of these respects?

Moses lived in the desert, not in a house of His own but in the house of his father-in-law. This was another school of humiliation. He worked for the man, stayed with him, ate from the man etc. May be Moses worked for no pay but the food, shelter and wife he had been given. May be you find yourself in a similar situation. Just like it was not the end of Moses' story, I want to let you know that this is not the end of your story. Things will change and change in the twinkling of an eye.

THE GOD ENCOUNTER

I told you every betrayal and rejection takes you closer to your Mount Horeb. And no one reaches mount Horeb – the mountain of God and comes back the same. After forty years of humiliation in the desert Moses finally stumbled into God at the back of the desert. Sometimes, it seems God waits for us at the back of the desert instead of at the front or in the middle of it. We need to go through the whole desert before we can stumble into Him. Yes, I use the word *"stumble"*. Moses literally stumbled into God. It was not in Moses' agenda to have a God-encounter. It was not even at the back of his mind.

I can tell you that someone reading this book may just be entering into his or her own desert. Others are in the middle of their deserts. But I believe there are some who are already in the back of their own deserts. In a very little while they will have their God encounter.

> *1* Now Moses was tending the flock of Jethro his father-in-law, the priest of Midian, and he led the flock to the far side of the desert and came to Horeb, the mountain of God. *2* There the angel of the LORD appeared to him in flames of fire from within a bush. Moses saw that though the bush was on fire it did not burn up. *3* So Moses thought, "I will go over and see this strange sight–why the bush does not burn up."
> *4* When the LORD saw that he had gone over to look, God called to him from within the bush, "Moses! Moses!"
> And Moses said, "Here I am."
> *5* "Do not come any closer," God said. "Take off your sandals, for the place where you are standing is holy ground."
> *6* Then he said, "I am the God of your father, the God

of Abraham, the God of Isaac and the God of Jacob." At this, Moses hid his face, because he was afraid to look at God.

(Exodus 3:1-6)

Moses stumbled into God while he was tending sheep. Not his own sheep but that of Jethro his father-in-law. Do you see what I see here? Even after forty years Moses did not have any sheep of his own. He had worked tirelessly for forty good years for Jethro, apparently without anything to show for it.

There is someone reading this who has been hunted for too long by the question, *"what have I accomplished in life?"* You may be asking yourself what you've got to show for the time you have lived. From the worldly point of view, Moses was a total failure. He had wasted an opportunity to become something, a mighty man in Egypt in order to roam the desert with nothing of his own to show after forty years of working.

The Bible says,

> 26 He regarded disgrace for the sake of Christ as of greater value than the treasures of Egypt, because he was looking ahead to his reward. 27 By faith he left Egypt, not fearing the king's anger; he persevered because he saw him who is invisible.

(Hebrews 11:26-27)

Why did Moses survive all these?

1. **His values were different:**
   "He regarded disgrace for the sake of Christ as of greater value than the treasures of Egypt."

You too must have a different value system in life to fully embrace and survive the adversities of life.

2. **He kept his eyes on the prize:**
    "He was looking ahead to his reward"
    You might need to ignore the pain in order to focus on the reward. When you think of all that Christ has promised you and focus on them, it invigorates and empowers you to go through adversity.

3. **He Persevered:**
    "He persevered because he saw him who was invisible" (Romans 5:3,4)

It was Moses' sufferings that produced in him the needed perseverance. And his perseverance produced in him character. That is why Moses became the meekest man on earth. Not because he was born meek but because meekness had been formed in him in God's school of humiliation.

THE BROKEN MAN

By the time Moses encountered God he was a beaten, battered and broken man. There are many of us asking for a God-encounter but unwilling to go through God's school of brokenness. We refuse to be humiliated but we asked for a God-encounter. We run away from suffering but ask God for a God-encounter. Maybe I say it again for emphasis. By the time Moses stumbled into God, he was a beaten, battered and broken fellow. His God-encounter was for his remoulding and transformation. It is the broken man who gets remoulded and transformed in a God-encounter. When an unbroken man meets God, it is for a complete chattering. Meeting God in an unbroken state is like having the stone fall on you instead of falling on a stone. Jesus said, *"Everyone who falls on that stone will be broken to pieces; anyone on whom it falls will be crushed."* (Luke 20:18) The one who falls on the stone gets broken but the one on whom the stone falls gets crushed.

What shows that Moses was a broken man by the time he stumbled into God?

1. **He considered himself unworthy to go to Pharaoh:**
   Exodus 3:11 "But Moses said to God, 'Who am I, that I should go to Pharaoh and bring the Israelites out of Egypt?'"

   Moses who saw himself as a mighty prince born to liberate his people now saw himself as no one worthy to stand before Pharaoh.

2. **He did not believe or even think the Israelites will listen to him:**
   Exodus 4:1 "Moses answered, 'What if they do not believe me or listen to me and say, "The LORD did not appear to you"'?"

   From the passage we quoted from Acts, Moses had thought before that his people would realise God was using him to set them free. But now he did not think they will receive his message of freedom.

3. **He refused to acknowledge his worldly wisdom:**
   Exodus 4:10 "Moses said to the LORD, 'O Lord, I have never been eloquent, neither in the past nor since you

have spoken to your servant. I am slow of speech and tongue.'"

What Moses says here to God is in total contrast to what is said about him in Acts 7:22. Not because Moses was lying but because he had been brought to a point where he considered all that as useless. Unbroken people depend on their natural gifting and worldly wisdom to be used of God. Moses had no such confidence. The forty-years in the school of humiliation knocked out the pride he had while in Egypt.

4. **He asked God to send someone else:**
   Exodus 4:13 "But Moses said, 'O Lord, please send someone else to do it.'"

   When God commissioned Moses in Exodus 3:10, it would have been natural for Moses to have gotten up to go to Egypt had he not been broken. Because of his brokenness he needed to be assured and reassured by God.

   * God promised him His presence Exodus 3:12;
   * God told him what to say Exodus 3:14,15;
   * God told him what to do Exodus 3:16;
   * God told him of Pharaoh's reaction Exodus 3:19;
   * God gave him miraculous signs Exodus 4:1-9.

People who are not broken run even when they have not been sent. They think no one else can do it better than they. They are angry when God uses some other person. On the other hand, a broken man sees himself unfit. He wants God to use another. He is happy when others are being used by God and of God.

May God take you through His school of humiliation to produce in you the needed brokenness, so that you will be fit for his service.

LEADERSHIP CRISIS

By this time Moses had "gone through" his wilderness experience. He had become one through whom God had demonstrated His displeasure against the mistreatment of the Israelites and expressed His commitment not only to see them free but also to see them enter the fullness of their inheritance. Moses was now a celebrated hero in the eyes of the Hebrew nation en route to their national heritage. However, it seems the man celebrated and acclaimed by the whole nation was despised by his own brother and sister.

The Bible says,

> *1* Miriam and Aaron began to talk against Moses because of his Cushite wife, for he had married a Cushite. *2* "Has the LORD spoken only through Moses?" they asked. "Hasn't he also spoken through us?" And the LORD heard this. *3* (Now Moses was a very humble man, more humble than anyone else on the face of the earth.)
>
> (Number 12:1-3)

Do you see that? The Bible says, Miriam and Aaron. Who were these people? Miriam was Moses' older sister, the one who had stood beside the Nile to watch what would become of her younger brother; *"His sister stood at a distance to see what would happen to him"* (Exodus 2:4). She was the one who acted as an intermediary between Pharaoh's daughter and the mother of

Moses (see Exodus 2:7-8.) So we see that she had played an important role in Moses' childhood and this led to his rescue or survival.

And who was Aaron? He too was Moses's older brother. By God's divine assignment, Aaron had been made Moses's co-worker (see Exodus 4:14-17, 27-28.) In a nutshell both of them formed an integral part of Moses's immediate entourage.

The Bible says, *"Miriam and Aaron began to talk against Moses"*. It means that it was not a one-time criticism. It went up for some time with the intention of continuing had God not intervened. May be you have been an object of people's malicious criticism. May be you are being railed and assailed by the sharp and challenging words of those who are supposed to be on your defence. Maybe you are being persecuted by the same people who were placed in your life to help you carry on with what God assigned you. Those who once did all to see you survive for some reason have turned against you. If that is your case I counsel you to stay faithful at what you are doing. Stay focused on what God has assigned to you. Do not respond to such criticism and so lose focus. God will fight for you if you refuse to fight in the flesh. God will uphold your position and authority if you refuse to fight with people committed to bring you down. Because Moses refused to defend himself against his assailants, God rose to his defence. It is quite a similar scenario that took place a few chapters later. This time, it was not family that rose up against Moses, but well known community leaders.

*[1]*Korah son of Izhar, the son of Kohath, the son of Levi, and certain Reubenites–Dathan and Abiram, sons of

> Eliab, and On son of Peleth–became insolent *2* and rose up against Moses. With them were 250 Israelite men, well-known community leaders who had been appointed members of the council. *3* They came as a group to oppose Moses and Aaron and said to them, «You have gone too far! The whole community is holy, every one of them, and the LORD is with them. Why then do you set yourselves above the LORD's assembly?»
> *4* When Moses heard this, he fell facedown."
>
> (Numbers 16:1-4)

What heart-breaking, spirit-damping, emotions-wrecking accusations levied against a leader. This was done by people who had been entrusted with much and therefore required with much. They were well-known community leaders, members of the council. In other words these were not outsiders. They knew the flaws of the leader. They were cognizant of the problem that existed within the leadership. Instead of seeing how they could amicably resolve the issues,

1. **They became insolent (V1)**
   There are many people who are insolent in their attitudes, others in their words and still others in their actions.

2. **They rose in opposition (V3)**
   People who were meant to work with Moses now rose in opposition against him. They abandoned what they were supposed to be doing.

There are many people today in leadership crisis. It may not take the same form but it certainly comes with adversity. If you are not careful about the way you react to it, it may lead not only to a breakdown in your business, job or the work God has entrusted to you, but also in a breakdown of your person.

The best reaction, if any is that of Moses. When he *"heard this, he fell face down."* Falling face down was not a sign of defeat but a position of intercession and listening to what God had to say in that particular situation. As soon as he heard what God had to say then did he speak to the people. Not to quarrel with them but to see how the matter could be resolved in God's way.

You have a place to which you can take all your pains, pressures and problems to; the presence of your Father and your God. You have someone to whom you can carry all your discouragements, disappointments and distresses to; your Father and your God. He cares for you and would provide a solution in the midst of the crisis if you give Him a listening ear. The solution may not be instant but if you remain faithful to the instructions He gives, you will have a lasting solution.

Instant solutions are not always lasting but when God takes you through a process to resolve whatever issue, He gives you the opportunity to learn and shape your character. Many in seeking for instant relief from whatever situation have ended up worsening things not only for themselves but for others.

To round up this brief study on the life of Moses, I will conclude that Moses was born in adversity and built in adversity. He went through all the problems from his childhood till the day he died without breaking down. The God who sustained Moses is your God and He will sustain you through every adversity if you allow Him to.

Summary

- There are many people who can only excel under adverse circumstances.

- The greater the responsibility you are called to carry in life the greater the pressure you will encounter in life.

- Adversity is hardly the making of the one facing it.

- Adversity is like chisel in the hand of a craftsman to cut away the unwanted portions and trim the rough edges, thereby bringing out the artwork.

- Adversity does not look at your face or form sometimes. It comes knocking at any door any time.

- The best way to handle adversity is to prepare for it by making up your mind in advance that nothing will ever knock you out.

- Making up your mind gives you staying power in the midst of storms.

- When God's hand is on your life, that place where people are drowning will be the same place where you will be preserved. The place which is the grave yard to many a vision will be the gateway to your rising to the palace.

- ✣ As a child of God you must understand that God has arranged your steps and stops.

- ✣ When God's hand is on you dead ends become bridges to the next stage of your life. Stumbling blocks become stepping stones to your destiny. Adversities become springboards to your God-ordained heights.

- ✣ There is a time when you have to rise up to life's challenges or go down permanently. If you must survive adversity you must learn to take the bull by the horn.

- ✣ One thing is certain; God knows when to close the curtains on each episode of trials.

- ✣ This is where many people blow it. They seek a natural solution to a problem which is supernatural in origin.

- ✣ Before you are celebrated you will first be rejected.

- ✣ Knowing that God is your companion and building that relationship is the only guarantee of making it sanely through Rejection Land.

- ✣ That cocoon is the reason you cannot enjoy life. Once it gets broken, life will be full of meaning once again.

- If you cover your sin, no matter how deep in the sand of life, one day, that sin will find you out. The sin which has not been exposed will find you out. Secrecy preserves sins instead of destroying them.

- Sometimes you are rejected and betrayed not because of anything you have done but because God has arranged a different path for you from that of the majority.

- People will not always treat you or react to your help the way you think. Some will be grateful. Others will react negatively. Others will accuse you of one thing or another.

- Sometimes until you are betrayed you cannot be fully and truly celebrated. Your betrayals are setting you up for a God-encounter. Every betrayal takes you closer your mount Horeb if you will refuse to harbour anger and resentment against those who betray you.

- The rejections and betrayals you experience in life are working in you the much needed brokenness if ever you are to be used by God.

- There are many people hiding in plain sight. Some are hiding from the realities of life, others are hiding from their past mistakes they've failed to deal with, still others are hiding from themselves and the challenges life offers. Yet there are some who are hiding from God.

* Sometimes, it seems God waits for us at the back of the desert instead of at the front or in the middle of it. We need to go through the whole desert before we can stumble into Him.

* You too must have a different value system in life to fully embrace and survive the adversities of life.

* When you think of all that Christ has promised you and focus on them, it invigorates and empowers you to go through adversity.

* It is the broken man who gets remoulded and transformed in a God-encounter. When an unbroken man meets God, it is for a complete chattering.

* Unbroken people depend on their natural gifting and worldly wisdom to be used of God.

* God will fight for you if you refuse to fight in the flesh.

* Because Moses refused to defend himself against his assailants, God rose to his defence.

- Falling face down was not a sign of defeat but a position of intercession and listening to what God had to say in that particular situation.

- Many in seeking for instant relief from whatever situation have ended up worsening things not only for themselves but for others.

Chapter 4

When Life Deprives you of the Basics: A Look at the Life of Gideon

*1*Again the Israelites did evil in the eyes of the LORD, and for seven years he gave them into the hands of the Midianites. *2*Because the power of Midian was so oppressive, the Israelites prepared shelters for themselves in mountain clefts, caves and strongholds. *3*Whenever the Israelites planted their crops, the Midianites, Amalekites and other eastern peoples invaded the country. *4*They camped on the land and ruined the crops all the way to Gaza and did not spare a living thing for Israel, neither sheep nor cattle nor donkeys. *5*They came up with their livestock and their tents like swarms of locusts. It was impossible to count the men and their camels; they invaded the land to ravage it. *6*Midian so impoverished the Israelites that they cried out to the LORD for help.

(Judges 6:1-6)

Some people are born into adversity because of the time in which they were born. Some because of the tribe, nation, or continent into which they were born. Gideon was born in a time of great backsliding in the land of Israel. And because of their backsliding they had to suffer under the oppressive power of the Midianites. Even the few righteous people in Israel were victims of the oppressive hand of the Midianites not because of anything they did as individuals but because they were part of a community or a generation that had forsaken God. Like I said before, some people face adversity because of circumstances far beyond their control. They suffer because they are part of a certain group of people. Though you may never have the choice of the adversities you face in life, you can choose the way you react to adversity. And it's your reaction that determines the outcome of whatever you go through.

I'll like us to see the effects of the Midianite oppression on the Hebrew nation.

The Effects of Midianite Oppression

1. **The Israelites became homeless:**
   "Because the power of Midian was so oppressive, the Israelites prepared shelters for themselves in mountain clefts, caves and strongholds."

   The Israelites abandoned their homes and built shelters for themselves in mountain clefts, caves and strongholds because of fear.

   You may be going through circumstances which have driven you from where you call home. The comfort of a healthy family life may be far-fetched luxury for you. Maybe in search of a better life you have found yourself in very deplorable conditions, and pain and tears fill your heart.

Do you know what it means to have lived in clefts and caves? Life for the Hebrews was reduced to that of the Stone Age. All the animals had to escape from their holes in the caves and mountain clefts because humans were now in great need for such places. How my heart goes out to those who may not be living in caves or clefts but are roaming the streets with nowhere to call home! There is nothing they can call shelter. The heat of the day and the cold of the night is something they experience without the faintest shield.

May be you are a widow driven from your once comfortable home by heartless in-laws. May be you are an orphan deprived of your inheritance by relatives whose only concern is the property left by your parents. In their battle for who gains what, you have been battered, tormented, shattered and disillusioned, and no one seems to care. Whatever the situation you find yourself in, God can turn that around in the split of a second, if you believe and act on divine instruction.

2. **They could not enjoy their harvest:**

"*3* Whenever the Israelites planted their crops, the Midianites, Amalekites and other eastern peoples invaded the country. *4* They camped on the land and ruined the crops all the way to Gaza and did not spare a living thing for Israel, neither sheep nor cattle nor donkeys. *5* They came up with their livestock and their tents like swarms of locusts. It was impossible to count the men and their camels; they invaded the land to ravage it."

Judges 6:3-5

I want you to take note of the words used here.

* The Midianites, Amalekites and other eastern people <u>invaded</u> the country. They penetrated every nook and cranny of the Hebrew national territory in large numbers. Their numbers were impossible to count; whether of men or of their camels. It could only be described as swarms of locusts. And when locusts invade a place you know what becomes of that place by the time the locusts are leaving.

* They <u>ruined</u> the crops. This means they did not permit the crops to grow to maturity. They allowed the Israelites to work but not to harvest. When they invaded the land they ensured that nothing was left that could grow to maturity to provide a living for the Israelites.

* They <u>ravaged</u> the land. Everything was turned upside down, broken and scattered by the time the invaders left. "They did not spare a living thing for Israel." All animals were killed. Humans who could not run were not spared either. What a destructive hand!

3. **They were impoverished:**

    "Midian so impoverished the Israelites that they cried out to the LORD for help."

    When a man is driven from home; plants and cannot harvest, rears animals and cannot enjoy of their milk or wool or any other produce, the effect can only be abject poverty. Theirs was a life void of even the most basic necessities of life.

It is in such an era that Gideon lived. He experienced first-hand the bitter consequences of satanic oppression. Like Gideon many have been forced to live like fugitives. They may be among people but they are hiding. They are certain areas of their lives that remain hidden in mountain clefts and caves to which no one is granted access. They have allowed fear to drive them away from the comfort of belonging to God's family. Fear of rejection, fear of being exposed, fear of failure, and fear of being misunderstood has kept many in a mountain cleft away from the normal activities that constitute a healthy life.

Others have their lives invaded by sickness and disease. Some have their lives invaded, ruined, ravaged and impoverished by demonic oppression. There are some who have been impoverished and drained emotionally by the pressures of this life. Others have been impoverished and drained psychologically by the worries and anxieties of life. Some have been reduced to social misfits because of the injustice against them. Whatever case you find yourself in, may I let you know that God is interested in bringing you out of it into absolute freedom!

God's Solution in Times of Adversity

The Israelites did one thing in the midst of all this. "They cried out to the Lord for help." When they cried out to the Lord for help what did the Lord do? Obviously He did not cause all the Midianites and Amelakites to perish instantly. He did not take the Israelites out of that land into a new land where these enemies could not reach. This is what the Lord did:

⁷When the Israelites cried to the LORD because of Midian, ⁸he sent them a prophet, who said, "This is what the LORD, the God of Israel, says: I brought you up out of Egypt, out of the land of slavery. ⁹ I snatched you from the power of Egypt and from the hand of all your oppressors. I drove them from before you and gave you their land. ¹⁰ I said to you, 'I am the LORD your God; do not worship the gods of the Amorites, in whose land you live.' But you have not listened to me."

(Judges 6:7-10)

1. **He sent a prophet to them:**
   God's prophets are God's tool for the liberation of His people from bondage. Israel cried and God sent a prophet to them. The Bible says, *"The Lord used a prophet to bring Israel up from Egypt, by a prophet He cared for him."* (Hosea 12:13).

   Egypt talks of the place of bondage, slavery and oppression. And God's instrument of liberation from every form of Egypt is His prophet. Have you ever asked God to send His prophet towards your direction? Sometimes God sends His prophets, but because we fail to receive them as prophets we forfeit the blessing and reward that come with receiving a prophet because he is a prophet. They "cried to the Lord… He sent them a prophet…" Pray daily that your eyes will be opened to recognise God's prophets and that your heart will be open to receive them with gratitude. The Bible talks in the book of Matthew of the prophet's reward. One aspect of the prophet's reward is deliverance. An encounter with a prophet sent from God is the shortest cut to total freedom.

2. **The prophet spoke God's word:**
"… He sent them a prophet who said, 'this is what the Lord, the God of Israel says …"

My brethren I want to tell you that your solution lies in the word of the Lord through the mouth of His prophet. The prophet is God's messenger. He is the mouthpiece of God to his people. He says in His word that, *"As the rain and the snow come down from heaven, and do not return to it without watering the earth and making it bud and flourish, so that it yields seed for the sower and bread for the eater, so is my word that goes out from my mouth: It will not return to me empty, but will accomplish what I desire and achieve the purpose for which I sent it."* (Isaiah 55:10-11). God's word will always accomplish its purpose of deliverance, freedom and liberation for God's people. God says of Himself as one *"who carries out the words of his servants and fulfils the predictions of his messengers"* (Isaiah 44:26). Your attitude to God's word in the midst of your adversity will determine the outcome for you. Believe the predictions of God's messengers and things will change for the better.

3. **He confronted them with their backsliding and disobedience:**
Many people try to provide a solution to problems before they have pointed out or confronted those involved with the cause of their adversity. The fact that God confronted the Israelites with their sin and backsliding does

not mean God did not care. When you try to provide a solution before the cause of the problem is identified and addressed, you are placing the cart before the horse and nothing but a wreck should be expected. Any such solution can only be deceptive and short lived. That is why you see one person going through a cycle of the same problem because a lasting solution was not sought. Are you interested in a lasting solution? Are you willing to confront the cause rather than the effect? Until the cause is handled it will continue to produce its effects. Confront the cause and that will be the beginning of your permanent freedom and deliverance and healing.

For many of you, your problem lies in the fact that you live in total neglect for the word of God. Some live in flagrant disobedience to established divine principles. For others it is the deep problem of ignorance of what God has made of them, still because they are not committed to knowing God's word.

When you begin to pay attention to what God has said in His word, if you begin to pay attention to and apply divine principles in your life, business and all that concerns you, then you are on the pathway to total, absolute and permanent freedom and wholeness. To an extent, the solution to your problem lies with you. You can decide to enter into it now by having and maintaining the right attitude to what God says.

THE LIFE-CHANGING ENCOUNTER

*11*The angel of the LORD came and sat down under the oak in Ophrah that belonged to Joash the Abiezrite, where his son Gideon was threshing wheat in a winepress to keep it from the Midianites. *12* When the angel of the LORD appeared to Gideon, he said, "The LORD is with you, mighty warrior."

13 "But sir," Gideon replied, "if the LORD is with us, why has all this happened to us? Where are all his wonders that our fathers told us about when they said, 'Did not the LORD bring us up out of Egypt?' But now the LORD has abandoned us and put us into the hand of Midian."

14 The LORD turned to him and said, "Go in the strength you have and save Israel out of Midian's hand. Am I not sending you?"

15 "But Lord," Gideon asked, "how can I save Israel? My clan is the weakest in Manasseh, and I am the least in my family."

16 The LORD answered, "I will be with you, and you will strike down all the Midianites together."

(Judges 6:11-16)

By now you've got a vivid mental picture of what Gideon was in. Surely Gideon was by now dejected, discouraged, disappointed, and disillusioned because of the intense adverse circumstances in which he found himself. But there is one thing to be admired in him; he refused to resign into a state of despondency. He refused to be relegated into the ravine of depression. Gideon remained at work, doing all what was in his power to get the best out of the situation. This points to the fact that men of valour are those who refuse to resign against the backdrop of hopelessness even in the most hopeless of situations. They do all in their power to get the best out of crisis situations.

Most often the thin line between triumph and defeat lies in what separates hope from despair. Hope is the lifeline in the midst of any ordeal. Depression never has a place in the life of the hopeful. The angel told Gideon, "The Lord is with you, mighty warrior." And Gideon asked a question many people ask. Some may not ask it out loud but their thoughts are infested with such questions of disillusionment. "If the Lord is with us, why has all this happened to us?"

There are many preachers today with narrow-skin-deep theology that says if God is with you, wrong things will never happen in your life. And this is just the kind of theology Gideon held to. He considered calamity and adversity as a sign of abandonment by God. Have you asked yourself that question? Have others asked you that question because of what is happening in your life? Do you feel forsaken and abandoned by the God you serve? Gideon felt that same way. But I want you to know that as long as you are a child of God, God is in you, with you, and for you no matter what you may be going through. He has promised to never leave nor forsake you no matter the circumstance. And for sure His word is always and forever true. May be you should shout it out loud to yourself "God is with me, in me and for me all the time." Meditate on that fact and let it sink deep in the inside of you.

May be I give you a series of verses for you to meditate on. I meditated on these verses over a period of two months, I assure you that it is important that you take time to meditate on each verse, stay at it as long as the Lord speaks to you through it. Write down what God says to you and reflect over it in the course of your day. There are some verses I stayed at for a couple of days before moving to the next verse. If you do this, then your perspective with respect to God's eternal presence with the believer will change positively.

Genesis 26:24 "That night the LORD appeared to him and said, «I am the God of your father Abraham. Do not be afraid, for I am with you; I will bless you and will increase the number of your descendants for the sake of my servant Abraham.»"

Genesis 28:15 "I am with you and will watch over you wherever you go, and I will bring you back to this land. I will not leave you until I have done what I have promised you"

Joshua 3:7 "And the LORD said to Joshua, "Today I will begin to exalt you in the eyes of all Israel, so they may know that I am with you as I was with Moses"

Isaiah 41:10 "So do not fear, for I am with you; do not be dismayed, for I am your God. I will strengthen you and help you; I will uphold you with my righteous right hand."

Jeremiah 1:8 "Do not be afraid of them, for I am with you and will rescue you," declares the LORD."

Jeremiah 1:19 "They will fight against you but will not overcome you, for I am with you and will rescue you," declares the LORD."

Jeremiah 15:20 "I will make you a wall to this people, a fortified wall of bronze; they will fight against you but will not overcome you, for I am with you to rescue and save you,"declares the LORD."

Jeremiah 30:11 "I am with you and will save you,' declares the LORD.`Though I completely destroy all the nations among which I scatter you, I will not completely destroy you. I will discipline you but only with justice; I will not let you go entirely unpunished."

Jeremiah 42:11 "Do not be afraid of the king of Babylon, whom you now fear. Do not be afraid of him, declares the LORD, for I am with you and will save you and deliver you from his hands."

Matthew 28:19-20 "*19*Therefore go and make disciples of all nations, baptizing them in the name of the Father and of the Son and of the Holy Spirit, *20* and teaching them to obey everything I have commanded you. And surely I am with you always, to the very end of the age."

Judges 6:16 "The LORD answered, «I will be with you, and you will strike down all the Midianites together.»"

Isaiah 43:2 "When you pass through the waters , I will be with you; and when you pass through the rivers, they will not sweep over you. When you walk through the fire, you will not be burned; the flames will not set you ablaze."

Deuteronomy 31:6 "Be strong and courageous. Do not be afraid or terrified because of them, for the LORD your God goes with you; he will never leave you nor forsake you."

Joshua 1:5 "No one will be able to stand up against you all the days of your life. As I was with Moses, so I will be with you; I will never leave you nor forsake you."

I Chronicles 28:20 "David also said to Solomon his son, "Be strong and courageous, and do the work. Do not be afraid or discouraged, for the LORD God, my God, is with you. He will not fail you or forsake you until all the work for the service of the temple of the LORD is finished."

Hebrews 13:5 "Keep your lives free from the love of money and be content with what you have, because God has said, «Never will I leave you; never will I forsake you.»"

The Ultimate Assurance

The one who is assured of God's presence, no matter the situation he or she finds himself in, remains invincible. It is the consciousness of God's presence that guarantee's triumph in any and every circumstance.

When Gideon became assured of God's presence, he threw away the cloak of cowardice he had put on due to fear and intimidation and gave room for the mighty warrior that was dormant in him to rise up. It was the assurance of God's presence that gave him the courage and boldness to, with three hundred men, wage war against the countless number of Midianite troops. You cannot rise to the realm of triumph and walk the streets of boldness and courage if you have not received a divinely imparted assurance of the eternal presence of the Almighty God in you, with you, for you and around you.

I advise you to meditate on nothing else but the verses I gave you until you are convinced in your spirit man of the presence of Him with whom nothing is impossible. With this spiritual knowledge all the false evidence the devil may present to make you believe that God has abandoned or forsaken you will fade and vanish like mist in the heat of a furnace. Be assured of God's presence in any and every circumstance of your life. With that you can sing with boldness and an uplifted hand even when you walk through the valley of the shadow of death, because you have ceased to fear any evil. Why? Because you are convinced that the Lord God of hosts is with you and for you!

Summary

✤ Some people are born into adversity because of the time in which they were born. Some because of the tribe, nation, or continent into which they were born.

✤ Whatever the situation you find yourself in, God can turn that around in the split of a second, if you believe and act on divine instruction.

✤ Whatever case you find yourself in, may I let you know that God is interested in bringing you out of it into absolute freedom!

✤ Pray daily that your eyes will be opened to recognise God's prophets and that your heart will be open to receive them with gratitude.

✤ An encounter with a prophet sent from God is the shortest cut to total freedom.

✤ Your attitude to God's word in the midst of your adversity will determine the outcome for you.

✤ Many people try to provide a solution to problems before they have pointed out or confronted those involved with the cause of their adversity.

✤ When you try to provide a solution before the cause of the problem is identified and addressed, you are placing the cart before the horse and nothing but a wreck should be expected.

✣ To an extent, the solution to your problem lies with you. You can decide to enter into it now by having and maintaining the right attitude to what God says.

✣ Men of valour are those who refuse to resign against the backdrop of hopelessness even in the most hopeless of situations.

✣ The thin line between triumph and defeat lies in what separates hope from despair.

✣ The one who is assured of God's presence, no matter the situation he or she finds himself in, remains invincible. It is the consciousness of God's presence that guarantee's triumph in any and every circumstance.

✣ You cannot rise to the realm of triumph and walk the streets of boldness and courage if you have not received a divinely imparted assurance of the eternal presence of the Almighty God in you, with you, for you and around you.

Chapter 5

Thriving in the Midst of Despise and Disdain: A Brief Look at the Life of David

It seems to me that all those designed for greatness are born in adversity. Adversity has proven to be one of God's most effective tests to bring out the giant from within. It is meant to bring to the surface virtues and gifts which will otherwise, sink in the sludge of indulgence. For Isaac, it was jealousy and opposition. For Moses, it was rejection, oppression and apparent abandonment. For Gideon, it was oppression, lack, and impoverishment. As we are going to see, for David it was despise, jealousy and betrayal.

Adversity comes in many different ways. And certainly different people are born into different kinds of adversity, some multiple. The scripture is silent about David until he is mentioned by his father Jesse, saying, *"There is still the youngest, but he is tending the sheep"* (see I Samuel 16:11).

For those who read between the lines, there is so much hidden in that statement. So much with a negative connotation! Even his own father despised him as "the youngest ... tending the sheep". Why on earth will the youngest be tending the sheep when he had seven elder brothers? He was not worthy of even being mentioned. He was considered an outsider until Samuel asked Jesse if all his sons were present.

> *10* Jesse had seven of his sons pass before Samuel, but Samuel said to him, "The LORD has not chosen these." *11* So he asked Jesse, "Are these all the sons you have?"
> "There is still the youngest," Jesse answered, "but he is tending the sheep."
> Samuel said, "Send for him; we will not sit down until he arrives."
>
> (I Samuel 16:10-11)

Make the Most of your Circumstances

David was known as the boy who was with the sheep. His entire boyhood was spent away, at least most of the time, from the entire family. That is the reason when King Saul needed him the Bible says, "Then Saul sent messengers to Jesse and said, *"Send me your Son David, who is with the sheep."* (I Samuel 16:19). David's name had become synonymous with sheep rearing. What a stigma. I do not know who is despising you and why, I don't know what your name has become synonymous with. May be you are known as the woman whom the husband left for another. May be you are known as the one who always does it on foot. May be you are known as the man whose children have abandoned or the child whose parents cannot provide for. Just as the sheep company was preparing David to become the shepherd of God's people, your adversity is a gateway to your destiny. Through David's interaction with the sheep he did not only learn how to shepherd God's people but also that God was his personal shepherd. Psalm 23 which is one of the best known Psalm came as a result of David being with the sheep. David learned to make the most out of adversity. His time with the sheep brought out the shepherd in him. It brought out the warrior in him when he came in confrontation with the Lion and the Bear.

Sometimes circumstances have made some people to appear as strangers in their own family. David was regarded as one. Have circumstance made you a stranger in your own family? Are you being despised to the side-lines amongst the very people you are supposed to feel welcomed? That for you is your adversity which you can bring the most out of; instead of sulking and being depressed you can see it and use it as an opportunity to accomplish much. David used his time with the sheep to write many Psalms which have been a blessing and an encouragement to hundreds of thousands in every generation of human existence for the past three thousand years and more. Adversity is never meant to destroy us but to bring out the best in us.

DESPISED BY HIS OWN BROTHER

To show that David's adversity was really intense, even his brothers believed he had to be nowhere else and do nothing else but keep the sheep company. During a time of war, He was asked by his father to take supplies to his brothers in the battle field and to find out how they were doing.

> *17*Now Jesse said to his son David, "Take this ephah of roasted grain, and these ten loaves of bread for your brothers and hurry to their camp. *18* Take along these ten cheeses to the commander of their unit. See how your brothers are and bring back some assurance from them."
> (I Samuel 17:17-18)

In response to his father's instruction the Bible says, "*20* Early in the morning David left the flock with a shepherd, loaded up and set out, as Jesse had directed. He reached the camp as the army was going out to its battle positions, shouting the war cry. *21* Israel and the Philistines were drawing up their lines facing each other" (I Samuel 17:20-22).

One thing I want you to realise is that though David was despised and side-lined by the family, he was still obedient to his father and still sought the interest and welfare of his brothers. Your attitude to those who despise you determines the effect of their attitude towards you. You cannot determine how people act and react towards you but you can determine how their actions and reactions affect you. Maintaining a right heart attitude of love and forgiveness will always cause you to reap the most and the best out of all forms of adversity. The adversities you face can act as a thrust to your wings to cause you to soar or as clips to clip your wings so you are not able to fly. You determine the effect of your adversities.

Let the Giant in you Arise

When David reached the battlefront, he actually got interested in what was happening. He wanted to know why the entire army of Saul's melted into hiding. David's interest aroused his brother's anger against him because he thought David had left the only thing he was qualified to do, to show interest in what was none of his business. He had left the only company he was fit to keep to come and spend time in the ranks of the important people of the land. And what harsh words he used to express his contempt and to ridicule David.

> When Eliab, David's oldest brother, heard him speaking with the men, he burned with anger at him and asked, "Why have you come down here? And with whom did you leave those few sheep in the desert? I know how conceited you are and how wicked your heart is; you came down only to watch the battle."
> (I Samuel 17:28)

Indeed, Eliab considered David unworthy to be where he was at that time-amongst Israel's army. His question, "why have you come down here?" indicates that according to his own judgement David was manifesting conceit and wickedness. Those who despise others will hate to see them in the company of those they consider superiors. They hate seeing or hearing such people even speak. The second question of Eliab's, "And with whom did you leave those few sheep in the desert?" was a question to ridicule and humiliate David. Have you realised that people who despise others tend to ask those questions in public that will ridicule, humiliate, belittle and embarrass them? These are useless rhetoric meant only to persecute a man or woman.

David may not have been a part of the army but his zeal for God stirred up the giant and warrior in him when he heard what the Philistine said. David might have been in the "wrong place" according to Eliab but unknown to him the lad was honouring a Divine appointment that would launch him into the path of fulfilling his destiny. You may be surrounded by people who find fault in whatever you do or say. People ready to manifest an outburst for no reason. If that is your case I will counsel you to learn to ignore whatever they say with the intention to hurt, ridicule or humiliate you. For David, in the face of such ridicule and humiliation, the Bible says, *"«29 Now what have I done?» said David. «Can't I even speak?» 30 He then turned away to someone else and brought up the same matter, and the men answered him as before."* (I Samuel 17:29-30)

There are people you must ignore and turn away from if you must succeed in life. Some comments and attitudes will discourage, demoralise and demean you if you pay attention to them or to the one who utters them. Learn to turn away. Learn to ignore certain attitudes and comments. They are meant to distract you from your focus and breakthrough. Had David wasted time to argue with Eliab, he would have missed his opportunity.

DESPISED BY SAUL AND THE PHILISTINE

When David made up his mind to confront the enemy of God's people in the Name of the Lord, he said to Saul, *"Let no one lose heart on account of this philistine; your servant will go and fight him."* (v 32). One may have thought Israel's army and commander-in-chief would have rejoiced that there was at least someone willing and ready to confront the enemy that no one else was willing to. It was better to lose the battle than to be in such a stalemate of verbal confrontation, running and hiding. However, Saul's respond was one of disdain and scorn; *"You are not able to go out against the philistine and fight him; you are only a boy, and he has been a fighting man from his youth."* (v 33).

May be you don't have the "experience" man uses for qualification. May be you are being disqualified because of your academic qualification. May be you are being disqualified by man because of your age. We have come to understand that God has a different set of values he looks at from that of man. Often, those disqualified by men are those God chooses. Man has always focused on the external but God always looks at the rightness and correctness of the heart. The Lord had told Samuel, when he went to anoint His chosen king,

> But the LORD said to Samuel, "Do not consider his appearance or his height, for I have rejected him. The LORD does not look at the things man looks at. Man looks at the outward appearance, but the LORD looks at the heart."
>
> (I Samuel 16:7)

You may not have that which catches the eye of man but as long as you possess that which catches the eye of God, He will lift you up and set you high where you ought to be. You may not have the stature man requires. You may not have the beauty man requires. You may even be lacking in academic qualification. But if you would offer God the right heart, you would be God's man. Now, listen to this:

> [41]Meanwhile, the Philistine, with his shield bearer in front of him, kept coming closer to David. [42] He looked David over and saw that he was only a boy, ruddy and handsome, and he despised him. [43] He said to David,

"Am I a dog, that you come at me with sticks?" And the Philistine cursed David by his gods.

(I Samuel 17:41-43)

David had been despised by his father, despised by his brother, despised by Saul and now even the philistine despised him. The philistine despised and disdained David for three reasons

1. His size (External physique)
2. His age (Experience)
3. His weapons (Equipment)

For each of these external shortcomings, David had an answer in God.

For his size, he knew he had a great God in the inside of him. For his experience, he had killed the lion and the bear with his bare hands. And for his weapons, he had the Name of his God.

A Blind Date with Destiny

If you develop the right heart attitude, there is a time when the scorn of people will only set you on the pedestal of divinely ordained promotion and notoriety. Sometimes the enemy's weapon will be used by God to bring you from obscurity to the limelight. It will take you from the backyard of the desert to the front line of earth-shaking and heaven-rending victory. The boy with the sheep became the giant slayer. If David had not been despised by the family he couldn't have had the opportunity to establish his résumé with the lion and the bear. Every adversity prepares you to fulfil your God-ordained destiny.

Even after David had become king, disdain was not over as even his own wife despised him because of his zeal for his God. It seems there are adversities, some may have to live with their whole life.

> As the ark of the LORD was entering the City of David, Michal daughter of Saul watched from a window. And when she saw King David leaping and dancing before the LORD, she despised him in her heart…When David returned home to bless his household, Michal daughter of Saul came out to meet him and said, "How the king of Israel has distinguished himself today, disrobing in the sight of the slave girls of his servants as any vulgar fellow would!"
>
> (2 Samuel 6:16,20).

Do not let the attitude of people dictate your zeal for the things of God. Listen to David's response:

> "*21*David said to Michal, «It was before the LORD, who chose me rather than your father or anyone from his house when he appointed me ruler over the LORD's people Israel−I will celebrate before the LORD. *22* I will become even more undignified than this, and I will be humiliated in my own eyes. But by these slave girls you spoke of, I will be held in honor."(vv 21-22)

WHEN YOU ARE THE OBJECT OF JEALOUSY

The slaying of the philistine giant was the beginning of great accomplishments for David. He was launched into the path of great military feats. He was recruited immediately into the national army in a special division supervised by King Saul himself. It is written that, *"Whatever Saul sent him to do, David did it so successfully that Saul gave him a high rank in the army. This pleased all the people, and Saul's officers as well."* (I Samuel 18:5).

David had become so successful that his success was independent of his assignment. He succeeded in whatever he was asked to do and rapidly climbed the ladder of military success. David had reached a point that all he did pleased all the people and Saul's officers as well. You know sometimes, and most often, there will always be people who are not happy with a man's progress. But in David's case his rapid promotion and ascend "pleased all the people and Saul's officers as well." In simple terms David had become a celebrity, a young national hero. Songs were being composed to celebrate him and a particular song separated David's friends from his fiends. In the twinkling of an eye some admirers were turned to enemies. David had become the object of royal jealousy.

If I may say so, it was David over the radio. David on TV. David in all the talk shows. David in all the recent releases. I am quite sure if whatever was released, whether as music, a play or a book that did not carry David's praise had little prospect of topping the charts. The women in particular composed a song which they joyfully sang and danced to the tune of sophisticated music.

> 6When the men were returning home after David had killed the Philistine, the women came out from all the towns of Israel to meet King Saul with singing and dancing, with joyful songs and with tambourines and lutes. 7 As they danced, they sang:

"Saul has slain his thousands, and David his tens of thousands."

8 Saul was very angry; this refrain galled him. "They have credited David with tens of thousands," he thought, "but me with only thousands. What more can he get but the kingdom?" *9* And from that time on Saul kept a jealous eye on David.

(I Samuel 18:6-9)

Do you know that there can never be greatness without enmity? The greater a person's accomplishments the greater the enmity he faces. You can never be celebrated without being hated. Those who are afraid of making enemies in life should never think of accomplishing great feats. Sometimes, and most often, your enemies are not those you have wronged in life but those who think you should never have accomplished what you have. There are those who think they should be the centre of attention and attraction wherever they find themselves and in whatever they are doing. And anyone who poses a threat to these is immediately labelled as an enemy. From that moment when David began being celebrated, "Saul kept a jealous eye on David".

Let God Be your Hiding Place

If you take a detail reading of this chapter we are on, you will realise, Saul's jealousy was not hidden. He tried to kill David twice (vv 10-11). He sent David away from his presence and made him commander of a small unit with the intention that David gets killed by the Philistines. The Bible says David met with increasing success in everything he did.

"In everything he did he had great success, because the LORD was with him."(I Samuel 18:14)

While Saul turned himself into David's enemy the Bible says, *"But all Israel and Judah loved David because he let them in their campaigns"* (v 16).

Jealousy is such a monster that changes a man into an animal if given the opportunity. We see Saul becoming increasingly obsessed, depraved and demented. He quickly turned into a psychopathic, maladjusted social misfit because of a young man's success. However jealous Saul became, his jealousy of David only helped in his self-destruction. If you are in the midst of jealous folks who try to ruin you the best assurance you can have is in the presence of God. That was David's secret. He survived all what he went through because the Lord was with him.

"Saul was afraid of David, because the LORD was with David but had left Saul." (v 12)

"In everything he did he had great success, because the LORD was with him." (v 14)

"*28*When Saul realized that the LORD was with David and that his daughter Michal loved David, *29* Saul became still more afraid of him, and he remained his enemy the rest of his days." (vv 28-29)

It is God's presence with David that brought about his great success. It is the divine presence which converted Saul's jealous intention into favor and great accomplishments. While Saul was burning with jealousy it is written that,

"But all Israel and Judah loved David, because he led them in their campaigns." (v 16)

"Now Saul's daughter Michal was in love with David…" (v 20)

"The Philistine commanders continued to go out to battle, and as often as they did, David met with more success than the rest of Saul's officers, and his name became well known." (v 30)

There are people who will never be influenced negatively by others' jealous attitude towards you. When God's hand is on you even in what your enemies consider to be their camp, God will raise someone(s) to defend your cause. Even in Saul's immediate family, there was a Michal and a Jonathan who loved David. In the midst of jealousy, David's popularity increased. (I Samuel 19:1-12)

The most important lesson I want you to note in all this is David's attitude toward Saul. He refused to retaliate or regard Saul as an enemy. He maintained a right heart attitude towards Saul by persistently refusing to take matters into his hands. He let God fight for him. You too can entrust even the worst person in the hands of God. Refuse to reduce yourself into the mire of jealousy, hatred and retaliations as it will only help to ground you and prevent you from soaring.

HAVE YOU BEEN BETRAYED?

It seems that as the times draw to their close, traitors will increasingly betray. Many will sell out in different ways for the gain of illicit favors. The virtue of loyalty which results from unity of heart will be a rare commodity, and this seems to already be the case. In this generation of get-what-I-want-at-all-cost, *"Brother will betray brother to death, and a father his child, children will rebel against their parents and have them put to death"*. (Matthew 10:21) Inner circles are increasingly being infiltrated by traitors who want easy ascent on the ladder of life. Some may not go the whole length to betray to death but what about other people's confidence? Can you keep a secret? Can you willingly reveal a confidence? What about the reputations that are increasingly being damaged by traitors willing to sell out for money? The Bible says, *"If you argue your case with a neighbor, do not betray another man's confidence"*. (Proverbs 25:9)

There are those who like taking unfair advantage of others. And one easy way to do this is to betray another man's confidence. Loyalty means you keep your mouth shut no matter what happens. Now I should not be understood as meaning you becoming an accomplice to someone's crime. There are many in secret societies who are bound because they have refused to open up due to oaths of secrecy. Never keep your mouth shut when it comes to exposing evil for the benefit of society.

Why are people increasingly afraid to confide in others? Some are harbouring guilt and enduring its destructive effects because they are afraid of confessing to anybody for fear of being sold out. Can you be trusted with a secret? Will you easily sell out for the sake of favors you will otherwise not obtain? Are you trustworthy? The Bible says, *"A gossip betrays a confidence but a trustworthy man keeps a secret"*. (Proverbs 11:13)

Let us return to our character under study. Betrayal is one other adversity David faced in his life. Some major incidents stand out amongst the many betrayals he endured. In one of them, David had gone for the rescue of an entire community from the hands of philistine raiders. He risked his life and the precious lives of the soldiers with him to save this community.

> *1* When David was told, "Look, the Philistines are fighting against Keilah and are looting the threshing floors," *2* he inquired of the LORD, saying, "Shall I go and attack these Philistines?"
> The LORD answered him, "Go, attack the Philistines and save Keilah."
> *3* But David's men said to him, "Here in Judah we are afraid. How much more, then, if we go to Keilah against the Philistine forces!"
> *4* Once again David inquired of the LORD, and the LORD answered him, "Go down to Keilah, for I am going to give the Philistines into your hand." *5* So David and his men went to Keilah, fought the Philistines and carried off their livestock. He inflicted heavy losses on the Philistines and saved the people of Keilah. *6* (Now Abiathar son of Ahimelech had brought the ephod down with him when he fled to David at Keilah.)"
>
> (I Samuel 23:1-6)

After such a venture followed by the victory and liberation accomplished, one would think that the people of Keilah will do all in their power to protect and support David. This however was not the case. They were willing to hand him over to his enemy so they could find favor with Saul.

9 When David learned that Saul was plotting against him, he said to Abiathar the priest, "Bring the ephod." *10* David said, "O LORD, God of Israel, your servant has heard definitely that Saul plans to come to Keilah and destroy the town on account of me. *11* Will the citizens of Keilah surrender me to him? Will Saul come down, as your servant has heard? O LORD, God of Israel, tell your servant."
And the LORD said, "He will."
12 Again David asked, "Will the citizens of Keilah surrender me and my men to Saul?"
And the LORD said, "They will."
13 So David and his men, about six hundred in number, left Keilah and kept moving from place to place. When Saul was told that David had escaped from Keilah, he did not go there.

(I Samuel 23:9-13)

Many people because of presumptuousness have fallen prey in the hands of traitors. Had David presumed that the people of Keilah would automatically become loyal to him because of what he had done for them, he would have ended up a dead man. It is good to always find out from God who the people in your inner circle actually are. Do not assume that because you have been good and kind to those around you, kindness would automatically be repaid to you. History is littered with destinies that were destroyed because of presumed loyalists. I read a little book offered me by a pastor-friend entitled, "Know your enemies, watch your friends" in which the author draws several first-hand stories to emphasize his point that trust is a risk. The account we have just read in the Bible is a vivid example. In my book "When all seems fading" I wrote how the life of Gedaliah came to an abrupt end and the future of many under him destroyed because of his presumption of who Ishmael really was (See Jeremiah 40 and 41)

THERE ARE ZIPHITES AROUND YOU

There are some who will take it upon themselves to spy on you and supply information to those seeking your ruin. It may not be because of anything you've done against them. Such have just been deceived into thinking causing your ruin will bring them a sense of accomplishment. I call such people the Ziphites.

After David had escaped from Keilah into the desert (see I Samuel 23:14),Saul could not know where David was hiding until the Ziphites took it upon themselves, to go sell him out to Saul

> *19* The Ziphites went up to Saul at Gibeah and said, "Is not David hiding among us in the strongholds at Horesh, on the hill of Hakilah, south of Jeshimon? *20* Now, O king, come down whenever it pleases you to do so, and we will be responsible for handing him over to the king."
> *21* Saul replied, "The LORD bless you for your concern for me. *22* Go and make further preparation. Find out where David usually goes and who has seen him there. They tell me he is very crafty. *23* Find out about all the hiding places he uses and come back to me with definite information."
> (I Samuel 23:19-23)

There are certain things the enemy would never know about you until one who knows you well gives him the information.

And the truth is that Satan has released Ziphites in believing communities to spy and inform on members. Am I trying to raise unnecessary alarm or calling on people to live in constant suspicion of those around them? Certainly not! But I am trying to drive home the point that not all who smile, dance, laugh and feast with you are doing so sincerely. Some aim at nothing but a means to get the most information that can be gotten to ruin you. You must therefore possess the spirit of discernment and be open to the voice of the Holy Spirit. Sometimes it's good to validate the friendships of those offering such in the presence of God before opening up. If it were not for divine intervention it is clear that this instance Saul would have laid hands on David, all because the Ziphites were monitoring his movements and informing Saul.

> On another occasion,
>
> *1* The Ziphites went to Saul at Gibeah and said, "Is not David hiding on the hill of Hakilah, which faces Jeshimon?" *2* So Saul went down to the Desert of Ziph, with his three thousand chosen men of Israel, to search there for David.
>
> (I Samuel 26:1-2)

These guys were bent on selling David out. Each time it was they who went to Saul to inform him of David. They had made it their duty to betray David.

In spite of all the betrayals, God protected David from being killed and he eventually became the king of the nation. What I want you to note is that David never repaid these traitors with what they deserved. If you have been betrayed, an attitude of love and forgiveness will set God working in your favor. Never harbour any grudge or unforgiving attitude towards your traitors. It will only serve to limit you. The betrayals of men only serve to advance God's purposes for your life. Saul came to a point where he realised that David's life was indeed hid with Christ in God. In his own words he said *"May you be blessed, my son David; you will do great things and surely triumph. So David went on his way, and Saul returned home."* (I Samuel 26:25)

Summary

✣ Adversity has proven to be one of God's most effective tests to bring out the giant from within. It is meant to bring to the surface virtues and gifts which will otherwise, sink in the sludge of indulgence.

✣ Just as the sheep company was preparing David to become the shepherd of God's people, your adversity is a gateway to your destiny.

✣ You cannot determine how people act and react towards you but you can determine how their actions and reactions affect you.

✣ The adversities you face can act as a thrust to your wings to cause you to soar or as clips to clip your wings so you are not able to fly.

✣ David might have been in the "wrong place" according to Eliab but unknown to him the lad was honouring a Divine appointment that would launch him into the path of fulfilling his destiny.

✣ There are people you must ignore and turn away from if you must succeed in life. Some comments and attitudes will discourage, demoralise and demean you if you pay attention to them or to the one who utters them.

- Often those disqualified by men are those God chooses.

- You may not have that which catches the eye of man but as long as you possess that which catches the eye of God, He will lift you up and set you high where you ought to be.

- If you develop the right heart attitude, there is a time when the scorn of people will only set you on the pedestal of divinely ordained promotion and notoriety.

- Every adversity prepares you to fulfil your God-ordained destiny.

- Those who are afraid of making enemies in life should never think of accomplishing great feats.

- Jealousy is such a monster that changes a man into an animal if given the opportunity. We see Saul becoming increasingly obsessed, depraved and demented.

- It is God's presence with David that brought about his great success. It is the divine presence which converted Saul's jealous intention into favor and great accomplishments.

* When God's hand is on you even in what your enemies consider to be their camp, God will raise someone(s) to defend your cause. Even in Saul's immediate family, there was a Michal and a Jonathan who loved David.

* He maintained a right heart attitude towards Saul by persistently refusing to take matters into his hands. He let God fight for him. You too can entrust even the worst person in the hands of God. Refuse to reduce yourself into the mire of jealousy, hatred and retaliations as it will only help to ground you and prevent you from soaring.

* Many people because of presumptuousness have fallen prey in the hands of traitors. Had David presumed that the people of Keilah would automatically become loyal to him because of what he had done for them, he would have ended up a dead man.

* History is littered with destinies that were destroyed because of presumed loyalists.

* There are some who will take it upon themselves to spy on you and supply information to those

seeking your ruin. It may not be because of anything you've done against them. Such have just been deceived into thinking causing your ruin will bring them a sense of accomplishment.

- Not all who smile, dance, laugh and feast with you are doing so sincerely. Some aim at nothing but a means to get the most information that can be gotten to ruin you.

- If you have been betrayed, an attitude of love and forgiveness will set God working in your favor. Never harbour any grudge or unforgiving attitude towards your traitors. It will only serve to limit you.

Chapter 6

When you Are Familiar with Sorrow and Suffering: The Example of OUR LORD JESUS

No one else in all of time has or will ever be born in such adversity like our glorious Lord Jesus Christ. Speaking of Him, hundreds of years before His incarnation, the prophet described Him in the following words:

> "*2*He grew up before him like a tender shoot, and like a root out of dry ground. He had no beauty or majesty to attract us to him, nothing in his appearance that we should desire him. *3* He was despised and rejected by men, a man of sorrows, and familiar with suffering.
> Like one from whom men hide their faces he was despised, and we esteemed him not. *4*Surely he took up our infirmities and carried our sorrows, yet we considered him stricken by God, smitten by him, and afflicted. *5*But he was pierced for our transgressions, he was crushed for our iniquities; the punishment that brought us peace was

upon him, and by his wounds we are healed. *6* We all, like sheep, have gone astray, each of us has turned to his own way; and the LORD has laid on him the iniquity of us all. *7* He was oppressed and afflicted, yet he did not open his mouth; he was led like a lamb to the slaughter, and as a sheep before her shearers is silent, so he did not open his mouth. *8* By oppression and judgment he was taken away. And who can speak of his descendants? For he was cut off from the land of the living; for the transgression of my people he was stricken."

(Isaiah 53:2-8).

May be I list out for you the adversities He was born into and which He lived through;

- He was like a tender shoot;
- He was like a root out of dry ground;
- He had no beauty or majesty to cause attraction;
- He had nothing in his appearance to be desired;
- He was despised by men;
- He was rejected by men;
- He was a man of sorrows;
- He was familiar with suffering;
- He was like one from whom men hide their faces;
- He carried the infirmities of the world;
- He carried the sorrows of the world;
- He was stricken by God;
- He was pieced for our transgressions;
- He was crushed for our iniquities;
- He was punished so we could have peace;

- He was wounded so we could be healed;
- He was oppressed and afflicted.

We could continue the list of adversities our glorious Lord went through if we read through the entire chapter. But for the moment I want you to go through that list again, meditating on each point for say thirty seconds. Do not read further until you have allowed your heart to dwell on each of the points above.

We can write volumes if we should examine each of the points above. For the purpose of our study we will dwell on two points, His rejection and His familiarity with suffering. We shall examine how He was rejected and see what we can learn from it.

HIS REJECTION

From His birth in a manger to His death on the cross, the Lord faced rejection of one form or another by different sets of people, for different reasons.

REJECTION AT BIRTH

6 While they were there, the time came for the baby to be born, *7* and she gave birth to her firstborn, a son. She wrapped him in cloths and placed him in a manger, because there was no room for them in the inn.

(Luke 2:6-7)

Right at birth the baby Jesus was rejected by the comfort and luxury of this world. The world through the inn-keepers rejected the baby even while in the womb by refusing to provide a place for the family. It was no coincidence but a careful design to demonstrate to the baby-King that the world system had no room for Him. The manger was not the best place for a baby. However the parents thought it was better than having the baby in the cold-dark open.

Nowadays there are many children labelled as unwanted. Some are unwanted by the mother, some by the father and others by both parents. They are viewed and treated as mere accidents into the world of the living. Maybe you are one such who was born to parents who never wanted you. You feel the rejection that existed even from your childhood and this has affected you.

There are children today who wouldn't want to have anything to do with their parents because they felt unwanted. This is nothing but retaliation and revenge. It does not pay to repay evil for wrong. Let God be your avenger. The fact that Jesus was rejected even at birth did not cause Him to stop loving the world for which His incarnation was made possible. The rejection at birth only helped to launch Him into the kind of life that the Father had ordained for Him. Your situation is not a coincidence. Everything has been arranged to give you the required experience that will help you fulfil God's purpose for your life.

Even the things, seemingly bad, that happened to you at birth were permitted into your life so that He, through your life can demonstrate the fact that in Him, you *were also chosen, having been predestined according to the plan of him who works out everything in conformity with the purpose of his will"* (Ephesians 1:11).

The *"everything"* includes your childhood rejection. It is time for you to open up so the light of God can shine into the deepest recesses of your being and bring you healing.

There are many whose childhood rejection has been coded in their system such that they see everything through the eyes of rejection. The natural reaction to rejection is hidden anger and withdrawal. Many with withdrawn personalities are so because of rejection in their childhood environment. Sometimes the best way to reverse the negative effect childhood rejection has had on you is to openly and sincerely ask the Holy Spirit to heal you of the inner wounds and hurts it may have caused you and then become involved in the welfare of others who may be in similar circumstances. You can seek to minister life and hope to children who may be facing rejection in their families, neighbourhoods or at school.

Like we said, the rejection of our Lord at His very birth was prophetic of the kind of life the Father had ordained for Him to live. In His whole life, and ministry rejection was very conspicuous. And ultimately He was rejected in His death.

REJECTED IN HIS MINISTRY

This episode in Jesus' life, He had been baptized in the Jordan. He had received the testimony from the Father to validate His ministry. He had undergone a forty-day fast during which He overcame the temptations of Satan. He was full of the Holy Spirit and had returned from the desert in the power of the Spirit. All these had prepared Him for a successful start and launched Him on the path to accomplishing His earthly destiny.

All this was followed by an initial acceptance as *"He taught in their synagogues, and everyone praised Him."* (Luke 4:15).

In spite of the power, the fullness of the Spirit, the heavenly testimony he had received, He met rejection when He went to Nazareth, His home town. (see Luke 4:16-30)

There is a principle which operates in the lives of all those whom God uses in special and outstanding ways. Their lives are marked by rejection for the most part. No one, it seems, can be fully accepted until he has been rejected. If you have been called into some special service by the Lord, I want to assure you that, no matter the power and anointing that may be manifested in your ministry you are going to meet rejection in several ways. History has it recorded that all of God's servants have met with this particular problem.

May be in your case you expected everybody to accept your ministry and support it. But now you find rejection increasingly preying on you. Human rejection is the pathway to divine acceptance and promotion. In this episode of rejection, the intention of those who rejected Him was to do away not just with His ministry but with His life. Sometimes those who reject you will go to any length to let you know your services are not wanted.

There are different reasons for which you may be rejected. For Jesus, as seen in our passage in focus, the reasons were the following:

1. **He declared what He was:**
   We live in a world where many people do not know who they are or what they were created to do. When

Jesus read from the passage and concluded by saying He was the fulfilment of that scripture, the people found it strange that someone would ever say such a thing about himself. The world doesn't want you to be separated from its state of confusion and purposelessness. Once you begin to distinguish yourself from the *"maddening crowd"* you become to target of jealousy and calumny.

2. **The anointing that was on Him:**
   The one who is anointed immediately becomes the target of satanic confrontation. And one of the ways the devil confronts God's servants is to cause them to feel rejected and so respond with withdrawal. Remember I told you the natural reaction of a rejected person is to withdraw. And a withdrawn person cannot be used by God to reach out to others in a very distinct manner. Satan had failed in his direct assault on the Lord during His fast in the desert and now he resorted to indirect assault on Him by human rejection. It was the anointing on Him that "attracted" the devil. When you ask to be anointed, you are also asking to become Satan's prime target.

3. **Familiarity:**
   The third reason for which the Savior–Lord was rejected is because of familiarity. It is a sad thing for people to become familiar with the prophet. Familiarity not only robs you of the blessing you will otherwise receive from someone, it sets you in a place to oppose actively or reject passively. Even after being amazed at the gracious words He spoke, the question, *"Isn't this Joseph's son?"*

was that of familiarity and it helped give them enough reason to reject the Savior. That is why the Lord said, *"No prophet is accepted in his hometown"*.

The effect of familiarity is rejection. They had grown up with Him. He had worked in the workshop amongst them. His parents were in their midst. All these contributed to the rejection He faced in this particular instance.

4. **He confronted them with the truth:**
Jews are very patriotic to an extent that they would not want the truth to be spoken. Here Jesus was speaking the truth about their lack of faith and the blessing they had missed in the time of Elijah because of their lack of faith. This confrontation of the people with the truth pushed them to the extent of wanting to kill Him.

Rejection awaits all who will dare on the pathway of speaking the raw, unadulterated truth. That is why you find very few ministries and ministers who will tell the people the blunt truth of the gospel and the cross. Increasingly, gospel ministers are afraid to declare the truth of the gospel because of the fear of rejection.

Has God called you to proclaim the truth? Then expect to be rejected. Sometimes you will have to stand alone because of the truth. Jeremiah had only one person who stood with him in the whole nation of Judah because he was proclaiming the truth to the displeasure of the political and religious leaders of his day. Those called to speak the truth are expected to live part or all of their lives in the dark tunnel of rejection and compulsory isolation.

So know that the rejection is not about you or your personality but about the truth you are called to proclaim.

REJECTED BY HIS OWN

10"He was in the world, and though the world was made through him, the world did not recognize him. *11* He came to that which was his own, but his own did not receive him."

(John 1:10-11)

There are times when you are rejected by what you have helped established. Sometimes a man is rejected by the children he spent his money, energy, time and other resources raising. Sometimes a woman is rejected from the home she has spent her life building. Sometimes people are rejected from the very business they founded because some people who have appeared from nowhere think they are getting too much benefit. Sometimes ministers are rejected by the congregation they have spent time building. There comes a time when what should celebrate you doesn't. Of the Lord Jesus, it is said that *"Through Him all things were made; without Him nothing was made that has been made."* (John 1:3) and that *"16 For by him all things were created: things in heaven and on earth, visible and invisible, whether thrones or powers or rulers or authorities; all things were created by him and for him. 17 He is before all things, and in him all things hold together."* (Colossians 1:16-17).

The world which now refused to recognise and acknowledge Him was made and established by Him. It was held in place by Him. Not only did the world not recognise Him but at this stage like at birth, it refused to receive Him. Though Jesus had the power to speak the world out of its orbit for rejecting Him, He never did so. He could have spoken out of existence the very things He spoke into existence but chose not to.

Many of us react very poorly when those we think should recognise us fail to do so. Sometimes we utter words and behave funnily, harbour negative attitudes which only lead to self-destruction. Some people cease to do the good God has called them to do to others because they feel insulted by lack of recognition. To always expect recognition is to be greatly deceived. It is a trap either into self-pity or anger. There will always be some whom God will cause to recognize and celebrate you at the right time. It is not your place to demand or expect recognition.

The Lord was rejected by the creation whose salvation and restoration He came to procure. Was that not enough reason for Him to have decided to return to heaven without enduring the cruel death on a cross?

You can continue to offer your services. You can continue to show the favor you are called to show even in the midst of the worse rejection. The pathway of rejection is not an easy one to walk but it is the pathway to great accomplishments and great promotions. When God wants to exalt a man He allows him to meet with rejection when he thinks he should be acclaimed and celebrated. When the devil wants to destroy a man permanently he keeps him on the pedestal of worldly applause and acclamations even when he should go through rejection.

REJECTED AT HIS TRIAL

From the time of His arrest, Jesus was rejected and deserted even by His closest companions: "*50 Then everyone deserted him and fled. 51 A young man, wearing nothing but a linen garment, was following Jesus. When they seized him, 52 he fled naked, leaving his garment behind.*" (Mark 14:50-52)

Everyone includes all those He fed, healed, delivered; it includes those who had pledged their allegiance to die with Him. They did not care whether they fled naked. Their interest at this point was running away not caring how.

In the midst of His trial, he was rejected three times by the chief of His disciples (see Mark 14:66-72).

The Bible says,

> *13*The God of Abraham, Isaac and Jacob, the God of our fathers, has glorified his servant Jesus. You handed him over to be killed, and you disowned him before Pilate, though he had decided to let him go. *14* You disowned the Holy and Righteous One and asked that a murderer be released to you.
> (Acts 3:13-14)

The Lord was rejected at His trial by the Jewish authorities who represented the nation before Pilate. He was rejected by the crowd when they chose a murderer and disowned the Savior. This means everyone rejected Him at His trial. We could understand the rejection of the authorities because they had shown active animosity towards Him throughout His ministry. But the rejection by those of His inner circle is what is heartrending. Even this paved the way for His death and consequent resurrection and exaltation by the Father: *"You killed the author of life, but God raised him from the dead. We are witnesses of this"*. (Acts 3:15)

THE ULTIMATE REJECTION

His rejection at birth, at the start of His ministry, His rejection in life and at His trial all combined amount to nothing compared to the agony of being rejected by the Father. The companionship of the Father in the midst of all the other stages of rejection had greatly diminished their effect on Him. He had never complained of being rejected. It is written that *"... as a sheep before her shearers is silent, so he did not open his mouth"* (Isaiah 53:7). But we fine Him on the cross, crying in agony *"My God, my God, why have you forsaken me?"* (Mark 15:34)

May be you are facing a rejection from a father, the Lord Jesus understands what it means to be rejected by a father. He felt the agony of rejection by the Father when He bore the sins of the whole world on the cross.

Having sailed through His life of rejection, we now turn to His familiarity with suffering.

HIS FAMILIARITY WITH SUFFERING

Isaiah described him as *"a man of sorrows, and familiar with sufferings"* (Isaiah 53:3b). And it is His familiarity with suffering I want us to talk about. There are countless people whose lives are stories of one form of suffering or another may be because of their tribe, social status, nationality etc. In a nutshell, many people suffer because of circumstances beyond their control.

They suffer not because they choose to but because they cannot help but to suffer. Should they have the choice, their lifestyle would have no intersection with anything that causes sorrow and let alone with suffering.

And yet we see Jesus, the Son of God and God the Son. The One by whom, through whom and for whom all things were made! The One who holds the key to the store house of the riches of the universe! He had the possibility of choosing to come into our planet like the King He had always been. But amazingly He chose not to. He chose, by His own will, the pathway of suffering. And from birth, through infanthood to His adulthood His whole life was that of suffering.

At the age of less than two years He endured the arduous journey from Israel through the sun-scourged desert to Egypt when His parents were asked by the angel to flee. Can you imagine the suffering that He went through as a baby? A few years later, He had to undergo the same journey when the angel asked His parents to return to Israel. Even before then while still in the womb, He had to endure the journey from Nazareth to Bethlehem. (See Matthew 2:13-23, Luke 2:1-6). As an adult He had nowhere to lay His head.

Maybe somehow, yours is a life familiar with suffering. Surely, it is never pleasant enduring suffering. But sometimes those entrusted with suffering get the greatest promotion in the sight of God. You remember that the end of all this was the exaltation of the Lord Jesus Christ by the Father.

I wouldn't get into the details of His sufferings here. We have examined His rejection and have seen what it led to. To better understand how suffering can help bring out the best in us and from us, I'll like us to look at the life of Paul, one described as "abnormally born".

Summary

✤ Right at birth the baby Jesus was rejected by the comfort and luxury of this world.

✤ Your situation is not a coincidence. Everything has been arranged to give you the required experience that will help you fulfil God's purpose for your life.

✤ It is time for you to open up so the light of God can shine into the deepest recesses of your being and bring you healing.

✤ The best way to reverse the negative effect childhood rejection has had on you is to openly and sincerely ask the Holy Spirit to heal you of the inner wounds and hurts.

✤ In spite of the power, the fullness of the Spirit, the heavenly testimony he had received, He met rejection when He went to Nazareth, His home town.

✤ Human rejection is the pathway to divine acceptance and promotion.

✤ The world doesn't want you to be separated from its state of confusion and purposelessness. Once you begin to distinguish yourself from the "maddening crowd" you become to target of jealousy and calumny.

✤ The one who is anointed immediately becomes the target of satanic confrontation.

✤ When you ask to be anointed, you are also asking to become Satan's prime target.

✤ Familiarity not only robs you of the blessing you will otherwise receive from someone, it sets you in a place to oppose actively or reject passively.

✤ Rejection awaits all who will dare on the pathway of speaking the raw, unadulterated truth.

✤ Those called to speak the truth are expected to live part or all of their lives in the dark tunnel of rejection and compulsory isolation.

✤ To always expect recognition is to be greatly deceived. It is a trap either into self-pity or anger.

✤ God will cause to recognize and celebrate you at the right time. It is not your place to demand or expect recognition.

✤ God wants to exalt a man He allows him to meet with rejection when he thinks he should be acclaimed and celebrated. When the devil wants to destroy a man permanently he keeps him on the pedestal of worldly applause and acclamations even when he should go through rejection.

✣ Maybe somehow, yours is a life familiar with suffering. Surely, it is never pleasant enduring suffering. But sometimes those entrusted with suffering get the greatest promotion in the sight of God.

Chapter 7

Made by Adversity:
A Snapshot at the Life of Paul

The hallmark of Paul's life as depicted in the Acts of the Apostles and in his epistles is suffering. Sometimes it was voluntary and sometimes he was just treading the pathway that had been marked for him. He described himself as "one abnormally born". His birth into the kingdom was no ordinary one, in the sense that he was born in adversity and for adversity. You remember how he was born, don't you? If you cannot remember then turn your Bible to Acts 9 and read of his abnormal birth.

At his birth (into the Kingdom) he was knocked down from his horse to the ground while riding at top speed. This would have left him paralysed for life. He was stricken blind at birth into the kingdom and rendered totally dependent on others. The first three days of his life as a baby Christian were spent in hunger. His birth into the kingdom was a baptism into suffering. The Lord Jesus said of him *"I will show him how much he must suffer for my name"*. (Acts 9:16)

He was called into a life of suffering! Some people are called into such a life. Everything about them points and leads to suffering. They have been chosen to demonstrate the fact that there are some who joyously endure suffering for the Name. This reminds me of the Late Professor Fomum. In spite of his academic accomplishments and social status, he chose the pathway of suffering. And indeed for him one can say he suffered for the gospel unto death. He consistently demonstrated that one can joyfully embrace and endure all forms of sufferings for the sake of the cross.

Maybe like Paul and countless others in our contemporary world you are called to a life of suffering. Every route you take lands you by choice or by design in the arms of suffering. Maybe for you each time you choose the easy way it lands you into further trouble. For you suffering may be the gateway to experiencing joy unspeakable. It may be the gateway to intimacy with the Lord of all sufferings. It may be the gateway to outstanding revelations. Your life, though one of suffering may be designed to provide inspiration to countless others, unknown to you. It may be the gateway to experiencing the presence of the Lord.

For the apostle Paul, there were several attempts to do away with his life. You can find them in the following passages:

- Acts 9:23-25
- Acts 9:28-30

- Acts 14:19-20
- Acts 21:30-31
- Acts 23:12-25
- He was jailed, Acts 16:22-24

He described his life in the following passages

4 Rather, as servants of God we commend ourselves in every way: in great endurance; in troubles, hardships and distresses; *5* in beatings, imprisonments and riots; in hard work, sleepless nights and hunger; *6* in purity, understanding, patience and kindness; in the Holy Spirit and in sincere love; *7* in truthful speech and in the power of God; with weapons of righteousness in the right hand and in the left; *8* through glory and dishonor, bad report and good report; genuine, yet regarded as impostors; *9* known, yet regarded as unknown; dying, and yet we live on; beaten, and yet not killed; *10* sorrowful, yet always rejoicing; poor, yet making many rich; having nothing, and yet possessing everything.

(2 Corinthians 6:4-10)

23 Are they servants of Christ? (I am out of my mind to talk like this.) I am more. I have worked much harder, been in prison more frequently, been flogged more severely, and been exposed to death again and again. *24* Five times I received from the Jews the forty lashes minus one. *25* Three times I was beaten with rods, once I was stoned, three times I was shipwrecked, I spent a night and a day in the open sea, *26* I have been constantly on the move. I have been in danger from rivers, in danger from bandits, in danger from my own countrymen, in danger from Gentiles; in danger in the city, in danger in the country, in danger at sea; and in danger from false brothers. *27* I have labored and toiled and have often gone without sleep; I have known hunger and thirst and have often gone without food; I have been cold and naked. *28* Besides everything else, I face daily the pressure of my concern for all the churches.

(2 Corinthians 11:23-28)

Take time to meditate on the passages above and let the Holy Spirit speak to your heart.

Summary

- Some people are called into such a life. Everything about them points and leads to suffering. They have been chosen to demonstrate the fact that there are some who joyously endure suffering for the Name.

- For you suffering may be the gateway to experiencing joy unspeakable. It may be the gateway to intimacy with the Lord of all sufferings. It may be the gateway to outstanding revelations.

Chapter 8

YOU WERE BORN IN ADVERSITY

Everyone born of water and of the Spirit is born into adversity. Adversity is often the rod of correction in the hands of the Father. There is the tendency for man to drift into complacency, sloth and indulgence and so the need for reawakening sometimes calls for adversity. It is a tool to produce character in those who face it. The Father often permits it to keep in check those who often lack the prowess of self-discipline.

Because man is fundamentally corrupt, there is a degree of adversity by divine design which every one of us must face at any one time on this pilgrim journey. Paul said, *"We must go through many hardships to enter the kingdom of God"* (Acts 14:22b). In other words hardships prepare us and make us fit to inherit the kingdom. They are tools that shape us and prune us and purge us of all what makes us unfit to enter. Here the kingdom of God talks of the power, authority and influence of the presence of God in the life of he who has endured hardship for His Namesake. The realm of kingdom Power and authority is entered into by those who have gone through adversity. Adversity is the school of testing and approval for a high calling.

YOU ARE IN A STATE OF WAR

Children born in nations which are in a state of war often experience a degree of hardship that those born in time of peace never experience. For the child of God, the day you decided to make of Christ Jesus your Lord, that day you enrolled into the army of the Lord. Every believer is in the army of Christ Jesus. The Church is in a state of all out warfare against the forces of darkness arrayed against her on every side. But the good news is that the outcome of the war is already predetermined in favor of the church. However, this is not a call to laxity and ease but a call to endure anything and everything for the sake of our banner—the cross. That is why twice in the same letter, Paul called on his true son in the faith, Timothy, to endure and embrace hardship. *"Endure hardship with us like a good soldier of Christ Jesus".* (2 Timothy 2:3)

"But you, keep your head in all situations, endure hardship…" (2 Timothy 4:5)

There is no soldier who in his right mind should expect an easy lifestyle in wartime. War makes extreme demands on those involved in it.

You are in a state of struggle (wrestling) with both forces of evil in high places and sin that besets around. So complacency has no place in the life of one who must maintain the upper hand.

> For our struggle is not against flesh and blood, but against the rulers, against the authorities, against the powers of this dark world and against the spiritual forces of evil in the heavenly realms."
> (Ephesians 6:12)

> In your struggle against sin, you have not yet resisted to the point of shedding your blood.
> (Hebrews 12:4)

The word struggle used in both verses should give you a picture of what you are involved in as a believer. You are in a state of war, fight like a good soldier.

Summary

- There is a degree of adversity by divine design which every one of us must face at any one time on this pilgrim journey.

- Hardships prepare us and make us fit to inherit the kingdom. They are tools that shape us and prune us and purge us of all what makes us unfit to enter.

- This is not a call to laxity and ease but a call to endure anything and everything for the sake of our banner—the cross. That is why twice in the same letter, Paul called on his true son in the faith, Timothy, to endure and embrace hardship.

- There is no soldier who in his right mind should expect an easy lifestyle in wartime. War makes extreme demands on those involved in it.

- You are in a state of struggle (wrestling) with both forces of evil in high places and sin that besets around. So complacency has no place in the life of one who must maintain the upper hand.

Chapter 9

SOME FACTS ABOUT ADVERSITY

IT IS BY DESIGN

> For hardship does not spring from the soil, nor does trouble sprout from the ground. Yet man is born to trouble as surely as sparks fly upward.
>
> (Job 5:6-7)

Affliction and trouble are not random events which appear from nowhere. The soil does not produce hardship nor does it sprout from the ground. This verse tells us that affliction and trouble are by design and will certainly come to every human being on the face of the earth. They may take different forms but surely they will come, often unannounced.

The purpose of the design is not ultimately to hurt but to bring out the best in us.

IT IS A TOOL OF DISCIPLINE

> Endure hardship as discipline; God is treating you as sons. For what son is not disciplined by his father?
>
> (Hebrews 12:7)

Hardship is a form of discipline to restrain and constrain appetites and feelings which may otherwise go beyond bounds. It is a tool of training in the hands of the Father to make us conscious of the fact that we are in a state of war. If not of the hardships that many people face, the tendency will always be to drift from the way of the cross to complacency. Hardships are bits to keep us under control. Face the facts, many believers are as stubborn as horses, if not more than. The Lord says,

> [8] I will instruct you and teach you in the way you should go; I will counsel you and watch over you. [9] Do not be like the horse or the mule, which have no understanding but must be controlled by bit and bridle or they will not come to you.
>
> (Psalm 32:8-9)

In order to keep us from straying and going our own way into eternal perdition, the Father uses the painful yet objective tool of hardships to keep us on course and in focus.

IT IS A TEST FOR YOUR FOUNDATION

There are many lives build on sand. There are many spiritual towers with inadequate foundations—castles hanging in the sky. Because God is interested in genuine things He allows adversity to come our way to test the strength of what we build.

In the parable of the sower, the Lord said of one particular kind of seed that

> *20* The one who received the seed that fell on rocky places is the man who hears the word and at once receives it with joy. *21* But since he has no root, he lasts only a short time. When trouble or persecution comes because of the word, he quickly falls away.
>
> (Matthew 13:20-21)

Trouble and persecution come to expose the depth and strength of our foundation. The reason the one in the parable quickly fell away is not because of the volume of the trouble or persecution but because he had no root. The life which stands adversity is a life that has developed roots and is built on the rock. Such a life stands tall and firm in the face of the most severe of adversities. To prepare for stormy days which are certain to come, build your life on the word of God. Let your choices, values and priorities be in line with what the Word says.

> *24* Therefore everyone who hears these words of mine and puts them into practice is like a wise man who built his house on the rock. *25* The rain came down, the streams rose, and the winds blew and beat against that house; yet it did not fall, because it had its foundation on the rock. *26* But everyone who hears these words of mine and does not put them into practice is like a foolish man who built his house on sand. *27* The rain came down, the streams rose, and the winds blew and beat against that house, and it fell with a great crash.
>
> (Matthew 7:24-27)

IT IS A MEASURE OF YOUR STRENGTH

The Lord Jesus said, *"Each day has enough trouble of its own"* (Matthew 6:34b)

The strength of a man or woman, boy or girl is hardly ever known until times of intense pressure. When adversity comes, it comes to expose to you your strengths and weaknesses. Your strength is not measured when all is going well and smooth but when things are roughest. The most honest of persons will overestimate their strength. It is the tendency of the natural man to think highly of himself than he ought to. So adversity comes to give you a measure of how strong you are. And the verdict is should you falter in times of trouble, it is an indication that your strength is absolutely inadequate.

"If you falter in times of trouble, how small is your strength!" (Proverbs 24:10)

IT IS A CERTAINTY

I have told you these things, so that in me you may have peace. In this world you will have trouble. But take heart! I have overcome the world.

(John 16:33)

This is a guaranteed statement. As long as you are in this world of mortals, the Lord says be sure to have trouble. It is inescapable! In fact if you are not having trouble, it is an indication that you are a dead man walking. The Psalmist cried, *"For troubles without number surround me"* (Psalm 4:12a). You are in the midst of trouble; some obvious and some not too obvious—some known and some unknown. But the good news is that in spite of the numberless trouble surrounding you, it is written that, *"A righteous man may have many troubles, but the LORD delivers him from them all"*. (Psalm 34:19)

"The righteous cry out, and the LORD hears them; he delivers them from all their troubles." (Psalm 34:17)

Though the troubles maybe numberless, though they be many, deliverance is guaranteed. Just like it is certain that the troubles will come to us in this world, so deliverance from the Lord will be our portion.

THERE IS A WAY THROUGH ADVERSITY

The best way to handle adversity is not the way out but the way through. Opting through means you are getting ready for the next stage. The Lord has given us the way through adversity. He says, *"Is anyone of you in trouble? He should pray…"* (James 5:13a). The way through adversity is the way of prayer.

Hezekiah understood this and said *"I cried like a swift or thrush, I moaned like a mourning dove. My eyes grew weak as I looked to the heavens. I am troubled; O Lord, come to my aid!"* (Isaiah 38:14)

He knew that the only way through for him was to call on the Lord. The Psalmist said, *"In the day of my trouble I will call to you, for you will answer me"*. (Psalm 86:7) Trouble should push you to call on the Lord and surely He'll answer you.

GOD'S COMPANIONSHIP IS GUARANTEED

The Lord said, *"And call upon me in the day of trouble; I will deliver you and you will honour me"* (Psalm 50:15). This is the out option – deliverance, when the Lord gets you out of your trouble. But sometimes the best way is the way through and therefore He has promised to be your faithful companion through adversity. And so He says, *"He will call upon me, and I will answer him; I will be with him in trouble, I will deliver him and honor him."* (Psalm 91:15)

This is the way through the trouble. You can be sure of His companionship.

Summary

- This verse tells us that affliction and trouble are by design and will certainly come to every human being on the face of the earth. They may take different forms but surely they will come, often unannounced.

- Hardship is a form of discipline to restrain and constrain appetites and feelings which may otherwise go beyond bounds.

- In order to keep us from straying and going our own way into eternal perdition, the Father uses the painful yet objective tool of hardships to keep us on course and in focus.

- There are many spiritual towers with inadequate foundations – castles hanging in the sky. Because God is interested in genuine things He allows adversity to come our way to test the strength of what we build.

- Trouble and persecution come to expose the depth and strength of our foundation.

- The life which stands adversity is a life that has developed roots and is built on the rock.

- To prepare for stormy days which are certain to come, build your life on the word of God. Let your choices, values and priorities be in line with what the Word says.

- Your strength is not measured when all is going well and smooth but when things are roughest.

- If you are not having trouble, it is an indication that you are a dead man walking.

- The best way to handle adversity is not the way out but the way through. Opting through means you are getting ready for the next stage.

Conclusion

I believe the Lord has used the words of this book to speak to you and bring you hope and encouragement in the midst of your adverse circumstances. One thing is sure, you are better off, and more ready to face the adversities in life than you were before you read this book. if that is the case, then spread the word of encouragement by teaching others what you have learned or better still, recommend the book to them, or study the book as a group and be a blessing. May you thrive and bring forth abundant fruit as a result of the adversities you have been equipped to handle. If you have never known the Lord Jesus Christ as your personal Lord and Savior, I encourage you to do so by praying with me this little prayer while believing in your heart that God is able and faithful to save you from sin and make you his child.

> *"Lord Jesus, I thank You for choosing to die on the cross for my sins. I confess that I am a sinner in need of your saving grace. Lord forgive me all my sins, wash my heart, and make me your child. come into my heart and establish Your throne. I will follow and obey You all the days of my life. In Jesus' name, amen."*

If you prayed that prayer sincerely, then Christ has come into your heart. You can share your joy with me by writing to the address in the front page of this book. Find a Bible believing and teaching church and be a part of so you can grow and be encouraged in the Lord.

Some Publications of Perez Publishing

www.ingramcontent.com/pod-product-compliance
Lightning Source LLC
Chambersburg PA
CBHW072009290426
44109CB00018B/2188